Fresh Takes on Using Journals to Teach Beginning Writers

By Jim Henry

SCHOLASTIC
PROFESSIONAL BOOKS

NEW YORK • TORONTO • LONDON • AUCKLAND • SYDNEY
MEXICO CITY • NEW DELHI • HONG KONG

To my mom and dad, Jeanne and Gene Henry,
my first teachers, who continue to inspire and su[pport my] dreams

To Erin, Todd, Anna, and Ross, who keep [me close]
to the important things in life

And to Grace, my best friend, who has always believed in me
and supported me as a writer.

ACKNOWLEDGEMENTS

Throughout 20 years of teaching, I've taught in five school districts, working with many dedicated teachers, parents, and administrators, all of whom have important stories to share from their work with children. I am grateful to many people who have influenced, supported, and enabled me to tell mine.

A special thanks to all my friends and colleagues at Lomond Elementary School and the Shaker Heights City School District. To Dr. Larry Svec, Dr. Lynn Cohen, and Judy Kalan, my principal, assistant principal, and secretary, thanks for your support. I feel it every day.

I will forever be grateful to Regie Routman. Her support as a friend and colleague has so powerfully affected my life. This book wouldn't have been possible without her. She pushed me on, believed in me, and always helped me reflect on my teaching.

I am grateful to Wendy Murray, my editor, for her patience and encouragement. Her flexibility has enabled me to balance my writer's life with my other lives. I am also indebted to Terry Cooper, Paul Oh, and all the folks at Scholastic for giving me the opportunity to tell this story.

Betty Cope graciously read most of my chapters and helped me discover my writer's voice. I am most thankful for her encouragement and friendship.

Throughout the process of writing this book, family and friends—the Coopers, the Pinkertons, and Spisaks, among others—have cheered me on. My brothers and sisters and their families have always been there for me and continue to be there. A thousand thanks for everything go to my mother- and father-in-law, Sally and Norm Schultz.

Edited by Wendy Murray
Front cover and interior design by Kathy Massaro
Cover photograph by Kalman and Pabst Photo Group
Interior photographs on pages 4, 7, 17, 27, 43, 45, 59, 64, 79, and 95 by Kalman and Pabst Photo Group;
all other photographs courtesy of the author
Illustration on page 28 by James Graham Hale

ISBN 0-590-43373-3
Copyright © 1999 by James Henry
Printed in the USA

Contents

Foreword

I've had the professional and personal pleasure of knowing Jim Henry for the past ten years. He came to our school district after working five years as a reading specialist in an Amish community in Ohio and, previously, teaching multi-grades in an Inuit village in Alaska. Over the years, I worked with him as a coach and colleague, supporting his efforts and marveling at his teaching abilities as well as his close, caring relationship with his students. His enormous energy, ingenuity, and good humor extended beyond the classroom. I quickly learned there wasn't anything Jim wouldn't tackle, including building his own house on old family property with help from many family members.

Jim is a hands-on, attention-to-detail, collaborative teacher in everything he does—from constructing an operating cider mill with his first graders to

co-facilitating his school's language-arts support group for teacher professional development. A born storyteller, he captures his audience's attention from the get go and never loses it. He knows a lot but is never pompous or authoritarian. He is constantly questioning and reflecting upon his teaching while maintaining high expectations and standards.

This book on journal writing is unique, practical, and invaluable to the primary-grades teacher desirous of teaching writing well. The journal, as Jim and his students use it, is not just for life stories but also for exploring other types of writing, such as fiction, response to literature, and news events—all of which are first clearly modeled by Jim. Jim also uses the journal to continually evaluate how his students are developing as writers of content and conventions and to set new directions for teaching.

Beginning with the first week of school and continuing each day throughout the school year, Jim models writing for his students— meaningful message making that involves emphasis on both craft and mechanics. His modeling is both planned and impromptu. He demonstrates writing in whole-class mini-lessons in which he writes and thinks aloud on the overhead projector. Just as often, he teaches and models as he conferences one-on-one in a "lesson-in-the-margin" of a student's journal. His goal is not just to teach writing but to make it a pleasurable experience for children. He states, "If there is one thing I want you to take from this book, it is that journal writing in the classroom can be the most joyous literacy experience you can offer children."

Much of that joy is visible in the way Jim and his students delight in words. Daily word work, strategy instruction in spelling, playing around with words, figuring out rules and patterns, and engaging in word sorts are all part of Jim's and his students' fascination with words. In deciding what to teach, Jim continually asks himself, "What does the child know? And how can I connect what she knows about words to what she does not know and teach a strategy along the way?" Teachers will learn how to create an integrated spelling program that includes teaching multiple strategies, creating meaningful spelling lists, engaging students in peer testing, learning high-frequency "fast words," choosing individual words for study, and enlisting parent volunteers when possible.

What teachers will love most about this book is the explicitness and humanness of Jim Henry. Jim describes a rich literacy environment where first grade students are engaged in reading and writing throughout the day. He takes the reader deep inside his classroom—what it looks like and sounds like, how he teaches and scaffolds, creates literacy projects, models and evaluates, cheerleads and encourages. Throughout, Jim describes his daily successes and struggles and how his teaching continues to evolve. As he interacts with his students and colleagues each day, he respectfully and graciously shares what he knows and what he questions. He writes the same way—patiently, deliberately, and with great gentleness and care. His book is a gift to all primary teachers.

Regie Routman, January, 1999

Introduction

I have been writing this book in my mind for many years. I used to think that you had to be an expert to write a book. Now I know that's not true. I knew that I was doing some effective teaching through children's journal writing, but every year, I kept modifying my model while at the same time convincing myself that I wasn't ready to write a book. Finally, I just started, and found that writing changed my teaching and helped me answer many of my questions.

Friends have expressed amazement that there is enough information to write a whole book on journal writing. Journal writing is not new. Teachers all over the country have used it for years to improve writing. In most journal-writing models, students write for a set period of time. Little instruction about the craft of writing or mechanics of writing takes place. I have greater goals for my journal-writing model. The range of my students is broad. The Shaker Heights City School District is a large, suburban district of approximately 5,000 students. In my K–4 building, there are more than 500 children—half minority and half nonminority. Located ten minutes from downtown Cleveland, our students come from affluent families as well as those that are on public assistance. The range of students academically is just as diverse.

My journal-writing program must meet the needs of many students, and it does. The journal is not only a tool for expository writing, but through it we explore a variety of writing genres, use it to develop an individualized spelling program, and in a context that is meaningful to students, we use the journal to study phonics and writing mechanics. Whenever I read professional-development resources, whether a journal article or a book, my enthusiasm for teaching gets a big boost. Often, reading reaffirms that which I am already doing. Rather than completely altering a style or method, I pick up a a few new twists or techniques to make my teaching a little more effective. I will be flattered if after reading *Fresh Takes on Using Journals to Teach Beginning Writers*, the same thing happens to you.

Journals In the Reading-Writing Classroom

L ast October, my first graders and I took a field trip to an
orchard and apple-cider processing plant. The tour
included a walk through a haunted forest. All the way back to
school, my students talked nonstop about what they had seen. I
knew journal-writing time later that afternoon would be productive.
I wasn't going to see empty pages or blank looks on students' faces.

*I enjoy a journal entry
with Kristen, Cortney,
and Tristan.*

That afternoon, I opened the journal-writing session as I always did, by modeling my writing process at the overhead projector. I included some reflections from the trip, hoping to stir up some possible entry points for students to use when they wrote. I made sure in this modeling to include examples of editing for punctuation and spelling. Some of the children commented on how well I had remembered to leave spaces between words.

Sure enough, there was a high volume of writing, providing many chances for children to correctly place capitals and periods and to show good spacing between words and lines. My students included elaborate pictures of the apple orchard, the hayride, and the spooky pumpkins hanging from the trees in the haunted forest.

Many children placed their journals with that day's entry in the "copy box," to be photocopied and added to their portfolios. In other words, it was "all" there—just about all the components of my journal-writing approach. Propelled by their passion for their writing topics, students attended to the mechanics of writing as a means to make their messages clear, and they elaborated with pictures to further capture this memorable trip.

Most Common Types of Journals

◎ **Personal** Most often, this is a first-person diary format, but it is not limited to this. Some students mix diary entries with stories. The personal journal will be the focus of this book.

◎ **Dialogue** The teacher and student, or student and student, respond to the journal through written conversation. Comments are often brief, informal, private, and direct.

◎ **Reflection** Students reflect on what they learned, what they still have questions about, and what they want to know more about in a particular subject or area.

◎ **Learning Log** The student communicates how and what he has understood about a concept or unit of study. Students describe their learning processes—that is, "writing to learn." Some content–area teachers take five to ten minutes at the beginning or end of a period for students to respond in their learning logs. Learning logs may be used in mathematics, science, music, art, foreign languages, or any subject area.

◎ **Writer's Notebook** Students keep a record of favorite phrases and words they come across in reading that they might want to use in their own writing. They jot down ideas, thoughts, images, anecdotes, observations, and memories for future topics.

◎ **Class** Observations about a class pet, plant, activity, or trip are kept in a common log and may be entered as a shared–writing entry or as individual entries.

—adapted from *Invitations* by Regie Routman (Heinemann, 1991; used by permission of the author)

Versions of this scene occur in classrooms all over the United States. Most teachers I know use a journal of some kind. The amount of time each week devoted to journals; the instruction that takes place before, during, and after the writing; and the content of the children's writing vary from teacher to teacher, and define his or her model of journal writing.

The Power of Journals

Children need opportunities to write, just as they need chances to read, talk, problem solve, finger paint, or work with wood. Practice makes the doing better. But why have journals caught on in classrooms, from kindergarten through high school? Why is their use so enduring and widespread? I think it has to do with their simplicity and their authenticity. Journals require nothing more than a tablet of paper and a pencil; they are authentic in that people from all walks of life have used them for centuries. Journals survive from 17th-century American colonists to perhaps the most famous diarist, Anne Frank. In a *New York Times* article, "Tell It All to a Friendly Diary: Four Centuries of Intimate Thoughts" (May 16, 1997), writer Michael Frank explores journal writing's wide-ranging appeal:

> While all human beings are endowed with an individual voice, an inner eye, or "I," that engages in an ever-unfurling dialogue with experience, not all human beings are equally compelled to preserve that dialogue on the page, but those who are, the diarists among us, belong to a surprisingly diverse group. Understandably enough, they can be writers, who turn to their journals for relief and refuge and a chance to rehearse new ideas, but they can just as easily be travelers, soldiers, scientists, housewives, lovers and students. . . .

I think teachers and children gravitate to journals because of this age-old pull to reflect on and record the occurrences in one's daily life. But believe me, the first week of school, when I pass out the journals—70-page spiral notebooks with "Writing Journal" handwritten on the covers—I do not expect that my first graders will clutch their pencils and engage in an "ever-unfurling dialogue with experience." In very little of their writing do I see evidence of individual voices or efforts to rehearse new ideas. Often, I see pictures, scribbling, and random letters. But it is a beginning, and it is what I expect to see. Whether any of my students will go on and write the 21st century's greatest work of literature is not for me to foretell. All I want to do is get them writing, and share a form of writing that is fun and purposeful and that answers educator Don Holdaway's assertion that "learning to read and write ought to be one of the most joyful and successful of human undertakings" (*The Foundations of Literacy*, Ashton Scholastic, 1979). If there is one thing I want you to take from this book, it is that journal writing in the classroom can be the most joyous literacy experience you can offer children.

▲ *Leah and Lauren share their journal entries with each other.*

Developing a Journal-Writing Model: Years of Fine-Tuning

Joyous is not an adjective that has always applied to my journal-writing teaching. I've used journals throughout my 20-year career, and I have struggled to make them work. In the beginning when journal-writing time was announced, students took out their notebooks and began writing about anything they wanted. When I did not feel that the students were writing enough, I assigned topics. Modeling how to write was nonexistent. The only direct instruction that took place occurred when I walked around the classroom fixing grammar and spelling mistakes, unwittingly sending the message that correctness counted most.

Later, after collecting the notebooks, I spent time—usually after school—responding to every student's entry. My comments served two purposes: to reply personally to each student and to address a punctuation or spelling issue by providing the correct usage. For example, while writing about a trip to the zoo, if Sara misspelled *animal* as *anemal*, I would write below her entry, *Sara, I can tell that you really know a lot about animals. Which one was your favorite?* I hoped that Sara would see this corrected version of *animal* so close to her children's spelling version that it would impact her enough to change the way she spelled it. I was too subtle in my instruction.

Journal-writing time was not a fun time for me. I can still remember staying late at school, trying to uphold a promise to have the journals back on students' desks the next day. I'd chip away at the stack of notebooks, struggling to pen a personal message that included the misspelled words: *jacket*, *trip*, and *store*. And while many students looked forward to my corrective messages, I did not see the improvements in writing that I was seeking. There were times that I couldn't or wouldn't stay late. Heading out the door, I'd feel guilty walking past those journals. I found that I could avoid it all by not assigning journals as often. And the children never seemed to mind.

Journal Writing: Making It an Enterprise, Not Just Another Activity

In his book *Joining the Literacy Club* (Heinemann, 1988), Frank Smith makes the distinction between meaningless activities derived from routine and enterprises that develop naturally in the classroom. Educator and author Brian Cambourne speaks of the need for "contextually relevant demonstrations," a necessary condition of learning, to be repeated again and again by informed demonstrators. Smith also contrasts "school activities" and "enterprises," asserting that a school activity exists as a way for a teacher to grade a student and thus compare her with others, while an enterprise is a "group undertaking whose purpose is self-evident."

For many years, journal writing in my classroom was another school activity dutifully completed by my students to please me. It didn't promote authentic student writing. I know now that one of my greatest challenges is to engage or provide my students with meaningful experiences. Meaningful… it sounds so simple, but what does it really mean? I have been lucky enough to have Regie Routman working with me in the district, and one day I asked her if she could recommend a book that dealt with developing voice in children's writing. I was searching for a meaningful approach to writing. Regie thought for a moment and responded, "Jim, just make sure they're writing about things that they care about." She helped me realize that journal writing can become an enterprise activity *if* I provide an environment in which students are making decisions, writing about topics that are of high interest to them. And that is my goal throughout the year, to develop a journal-writing routine that cultivates in my students an enthusiasm about writing. This spirit of writing has to be developed slowly. It takes time and care to build into an enterprise.

Children naturally have so much to say with their writing, and they will say it if they feel they have listeners and a gentle coach to help move them along. While anyone can toss a baseball, add in encouragement and demonstrations from a mentor, and a pitcher emerges. Now I focus on the young writer and what he wants to communicate and use demonstration lessons to teach skills and mechanics directly. These demonstration lessons are a key piece of my journal-writing program that was missing in my earlier models.

Three Parts of Every Lesson: Modeling, Independent Work, Sharing

In the last few years, my teaching approach has evolved so that all of my lessons, including journal writing, are comprised of three main components: modeling, independent-work time, and sharing. This format of instruction permits me to set up an environment containing specific conditions for learning (see box, *Brian Cambourne's Seven Conditions of Learning* on page 14). The three sections of my journal-writing model have clear beginning and ending points:

- **The modeling session** is characterized by my standing at the overhead projector with the children at their seats.

- **The independent-work time** follows, during which time students work in their seats while I walk around to all the tables.

- **The sharing time** allows for children to walk around with their journals, reading their work to classmates of their choice.

Having a routine has been helpful to my students. There is never any question about the sequence. Journal writing takes place on Monday, Wednesday, and Friday, for 30 minutes each day, a routine that begins with the first week of school. Throughout the year, I do make changes as to how certain things are done within each section, but the sections remain. I should also add that children write independently every day while I provide guided reading instruction with small groups of students. It has been well-documented that writing is a big component of successful beginning-reading programs (Adams, 1990; Chall, 1967; Strickland, 1984).

Modeling

The Right Mix of Storytelling and Direct Instruction

Many of my students would contend that my modeling is the best part of journal writing. For five minutes, balancing storytelling with writing, I share glimpses of my family's life. Students rarely see their teacher outside of school, so when they get a chance to hear about my three-year-old son, Ross, pushing his lawn mower through puddles, or me chasing raccoons from bird feeders in my pajamas, they sit spellbound. Writing about my simple daily adventures

▲ *I model punctuation use while drafting a piece about sledding behind my house.*

encourages children to explore similar writing topics. In her landmark book *Invitations* (Heinemann, 1991), Regie Routman notes that:

> Teachers who use journal writing have found that when they are sensitive and respectful of students' attitudes, life stories, and learning processes, the children come to value and enjoy journal writing, and journals become an integral part of the curriculum.…Children are full of stories, regardless of their backgrounds, but many of them don't know they have stories to tell. An encouraging teacher can help bring out children's stories and celebrate them. In doing so, we affirm our students, build their self-esteem, and encourage them as writers. Students and teachers also grow to know and respect one another, and a sense of community builds.

You do not need to have storytelling talent to hold your students' interest. Share affecting and amusing events from your life, and your students will be enthralled. What does take some practice, however, is balancing the storytelling with the direct instruction you want to cover. Here and throughout this book, I'll give you play-by-plays to show you what I do during the modeling phase:

Standing at the overhead projector before my class, I present myself to kids as a writer facing a bunch of decisions: What topic should I write about? How are certain words spelled? What do I do if I can't spell something? What is a good word for a certain feeling? The questions spring forth one after another. I answer these "writer's questions" in front of the children, often in collaboration with them. And I admit, there is often some hamming it up involved. For example,

with a perplexed look on my face, I might appeal to my students for help. "Greg, help me think of a more exciting word than *nice* to use in this sentence" or "Josh, I need a period somewhere. Where do you think it goes?" And so, children's knowledge of written language is built, story by story, word by word.

Five Minutes of Modeling

I keep my demonstrations brief. Out of the entire 30-minute journal session, I give myself just five minutes to model. I want to devote the majority of journal time to children's own writing. I even set a kitchen timer, and when the bell rings, that's it. In honor of this brevity, students don't interrupt, because they know that it wouldn't be fair to take up some of Mr. Henry's precious writing time.

After the timer goes off, I wrap up the modeling phase by reading aloud what I've drafted. This often leads to a few minutes of revising, for in rereading, the students and I catch awkward language, misspellings, and so forth. Then I turn off the overhead projector, roll the cart back to the corner of the classroom, and students make final preparations for independent writing.

Brian Cambourne's Seven Conditions of Learning

In his book *The Whole Story: Natural Learning and the Acquisition of Literacy in the Classroom* (Ashton Scholastic, 1988), Brian Cambourne defines conditions of learning that all children rely on when learning to talk and write:

◎ **Immersion** Learners need to be immersed in texts of all kinds.

◎ **Demonstration** Learners need to receive many demonstrations of how texts are constructed and used.

◎ **Expectation** Expectations of those to whom learners are bonded (parents, older siblings, teachers) are powerful coercers of behavior.

◎ **Responsibility** Learners need to make their own decisions about when, how, and what "bits" to learn in any learning task. Learners who lose the ability to make decisions are "depowered."

◎ **Use** Learners need time and opportunity to use, employ, and practice their developing control in functional, realistic, non-artificial ways.

◎ **Approximation** Learners must be free to approximate the desired model—mistakes are essential for learning to occur.

◎ **Response** Learners must receive feedback from exchanges with more knowledgeable others. Response must be relevant, appropriate, timely, readily available, nonthreatening, with no strings attached.

Targeting Instruction

Within five minutes of modeling, I am able to address the developmental levels or phases of writing, spelling, language, and reading that we should expect our students to pass through on their way to becoming proficient writers. In every class, there is a range of students operating within these different levels, requiring varied instruction. Some students may need help with beginning sounds, while others struggle over various vowel combinations. Some children change their topics frequently and write with little depth, while others develop a single topic and show signs of defining a voice. The direct instruction that I provide in modeling is often focused toward students of specific developmental writing levels. For example, one day I might emphasize beginning and ending sounds of words. On another day, I will address proficient writers and demonstrate how to use quotation marks and an exclamation point as I recount my daughter, Anna's, first goal in soccer.

Independent-Writing Time

My Role as a Coach

After my demonstration, when I see that all my students have their journals open and their papers dated, I announce, "Pencils up!" Children then raise their pencils to the air, and with this action, I am confident of two things: 1. Students are attentive to the beginning of writing time, and 2. Everyone has a

Defining "Revision"

For my first graders, the concepts of revising and editing are interchangeable. To them, revising is simply reading aloud their writing to a friend and making sure that the intended message is present. In the course of rereading, spelling errors, mistakes in usage of capitals and periods, and missing words are caught.

"Pencils up!" signals that students are ready to write.

pencil for writing. I dramatically crank the kitchen timer and say, "Begin!" I may also remind them that I will give them a few minutes to start writing before I make my rounds, during which time I find out about the new exciting things in their lives.

As I make my way around, I read each child's writing from over her shoulder. I often offer a positive comment about the content, such as, "Oh, your Grandma came to visit. How long will she be staying with you?" or "I like how you described that fire truck as being clangy and ear-shattering. I can almost hear it going right by the house." This sends important messages to the student: *You have been successful in your writing efforts, because "Look, I can read it!"* and *I am interested in what you are writing.* I leave each writer with encouragement to keep going: "I can't wait until I come back and find out what happened to that dog."

Early in the year, I often can't decipher emergent writers' random letters and/or strings of beginning letters. But I know that there is a message there, and so I encourage them to share it by reading it aloud. Often, their fingers skim across the page while their eyes remain fixed on me. I write down what the child says in the side or bottom margin in a quick script form.

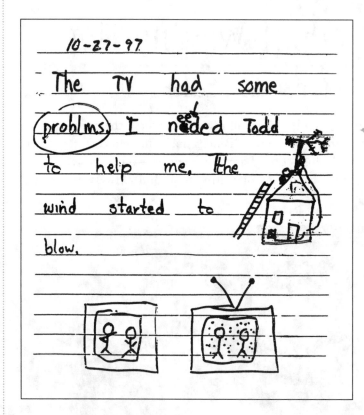

One of my typical journal-writing entries, which I compose at the overhead projector.

Making Emergent Writers Feel Competent

I use a pencil while taking dictation, never a pen or a marker. I do not want to send the message that their writing is wrong and that my writing is a corrected version. When I ask a child to reread his story to me, I do everything I can to shift the attention away from my transcribing. I encourage the student to reveal the fullness of her story by saying things like "Tell me what's happening in the

picture. Tell me more." I ask questions such as "What details would you like to add? What did the house look like?"

So, why do I take the time to transcribe on students' papers? There are a couple of reasons: 1. I may need to refer back to this page at a later date and remind the student, the parent, or myself what this writing was about, and 2. For assessment purposes, I want a record that this writing was in random letters. If it contained some beginning sounds, I want to record which sounds were correctly matched with letters. All of this information will help me to diagnose the current developmental stage of the writer.

Sharing Time: An Opportunity for Editing

When the timer rings after 10 to 15 minutes, students have two options: They can finish writing down a thought or share their writing with classmates. Because it's too much to expect first graders to proofread their work by themselves, I use sharing time as an opportunity for editing (see page 41).

I ring the timer bell to end sharing time when I have observed that most of the children have had a chance to share with several friends. This usually does not last longer than five minutes.

Johnie shares special journal memories with Harry.

Guidelines for Independent Writing Time

I work hard to keep the writing time free from distractions. I want children to be thinking, "Mr. Henry wants me to get all my ideas down now; later, after the bell rings, we'll work on fixing it up." I don't think of journal writing as a warm and fuzzy time when students are given, in the interests of fostering creativity, greater freedom to walk and sit wherever they want. Writers need to concentrate, and a classroom atmosphere must encourage this. So, when my modeling time is over and the timer has been set to signal the beginning of writing, I have a few rules:

◎ no wandering the room

◎ no drinks at the fountain

◎ no pencil sharpening

◎ no getting up to check a spelling resource; there will be time for that later

◎ avoid erasing—it takes up too much time; cross out mistakes, and continue on

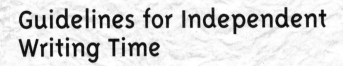

Invitation Time

Keeping the Writing Fever Burning

Journal time is not the only time that independent writing takes place. "Invitation time" is equally as powerful as journal writing. This is, again, choice time for students. This is a 40-minute block that I provide four times a week for the class while I am working with small reading groups. It usually follows a shared-reading or a journal-writing time, when I demonstrate and model reading or writing at the back of the classroom. I value the time I have with my small reading groups, but I am determined that the rest of the class be involved with more than just busy work. I am always amazed each fall with the range of abilities of first grade students. To meet such diverse needs, I provide open-ended activities. In the beginning of the year, students choose among topics and projects we've developed during shared writing. I stress the word "developed," because it's crucial that students work on writing projects that arise out of a lot of scaffolding by me and peer collaboration. There is no way I could assign my kids a topic and have them succeed independently—then chaos *would* ensue. The invitation-time projects always begin with my modeling the process. For example, a project kids created during invitation time originated from shared reading and rewriting of *Yuck Soup!* by Joy Cowley.

Yuck Soup!

In go some rocks.
In go some pencils.
In go some shoes.
In go some thistles.
In go some toothbrushes.
Yuck!

A Typical Weekly Schedule

Monday	Tuesday	Wednesday	Thursday	Friday
School Starts 9:05	Music 9:20-9:50	Calendar	Calendar	Calendar
Phys. Ed. 30 min.	Shared Reading 25 min.	Shared Reading 25 min.	Shared Reading 20-25 min.	Shared Reading 20-25 min.
Calendar	Invitations 60 min.	Invitations 60 min.	Music 30 min.	Invitations 60 min.
Journals 30 min.		Phys. Ed. 30 min.	Invitations 60 min.	Sharing 20-25 min.
Spelling 50 min.	Sharing 20 min.	Sharing 20 min.	Sharing 20 min.	Phys. Ed. 30 min.
				Journals 30 min.

		Lunch 50 minutes		
		Quiet Reading 15 minutes		

Monday	Tuesday	Wednesday	Thursday	Friday
Math/Science 55 min.	Library 30 min.	Journals 30 min.	Math 60 min.	Spelling 45 min.
Handwriting 15 min.	Math/Science/ Social Studies 90 min.	Math 55 min.	Science/Social Studies	Science/ Social Studies 60 min.
Art 2:10-3:00	Portfolio 15-20 min.		Portfolios	
Handwriting 15 min.		Computer 40 min.		Free Exploration Time
Dismissal 3:25	Go Over Homework		Go Over Homework	

▲ *This weekly schedule changes throughout the year. Deciding how to schedule all the subjects each week is still one of my more difficult tasks.*

"Yuck Cake" and Other Writerly Ventures

The children love the strong pictures supporting the print and the notion of concocting strange soup. We talk about how the story has a pattern—("In go some _____ ")—and how the pattern in this book and in so many others changes with the last page. I mention how fun it would be to make our own rendition of *Yuck Soup!* Before long, we have composed a list of "yucky" things that could go into a new story line. The kids examine the physical construction of the published version and discover it's produced with folded paper and staples.

▲ *Marquez proudly shares a finished book project from his portfolio.*

"Hey, we can do that!" they exclaim. And we do, with the aid of a long-armed stapler. Next, I choose five new ingredients from our class-generated list, and soon we have a new story called "Yuck Cake." I'm sure to make some children disappointed when I make the five selections for our class book myself—a deliberate act of selfishness, as I know that this makes my 24 pint-size authors eager to write their own versions. Some children borrow ideas from the class-generated list of ingredients, while others concoct their own wild recipes.

Offering Several Selections

Book projects like *Yuck Soup!* are just one choice, of course. Students can choose how to use this period, drawing ideas from my invitation list, which I write on the board. Early in the year, the list might look like this:

◉ Quiet Reading

◉ Yuck Book

◉ Journals

◉ Letter to Bob and Martha (our class box turtles)

Not all the activities on the list have to be visited every day, with the exception of Quiet Reading, an opportunity to read books of choice silently. I encourage all my students to spend part of their time reading.

I remember how risky it at first seemed to provide first graders with choice. Surely, it was an invitation to loss of control, chaos. I worried about a backlash from parents. But discipline problems declined. Easing students into the process by limiting their choices early in the year probably helped a lot. Parent feedback was positive, because students shared their excitement about invitation time at home.

Sharing Work With Peers

As the invitation-time projects developed, I started a portfolio system to house students' work. It was from these portfolios that children chose books and other writing to share with the class and parents. I set up a sharing system, too, so each student could count on reading aloud their work each week.

We store portfolios in two boxes that are accessible to children. Sharing time takes place in the open floor space in the back of the classroom, where storytime, shared reading, calendar, and math sharing all occur. On a bulletin board, each child's name is posted next to a straight pin. Four large, dry macaroni noodles fit over the pins of the four students who are scheduled to share that day. For the rest of the class, looking ahead on the list helps them prepare for their moment in the spotlight. After a project is shared, the author chooses two students to provide feedback to his work—someone to offer positive comments and another to offer constructive suggestions.

▲ *Andreas reads from his invitation-time project. Classmates enjoy his story and pick up new ideas for future projects.*

Ongoing Modeling

As the year progresses, I model books and poems with more complex patterns. Often, ideas for writing naturally develop from story time. For example, after reading the book *Animals Should Definitely Not Wear Clothing* by Judi and Ron Barrett, I said to students, "This is a good book. I bet I could make a book called *Animals Should Definitely Not Go to School.*" Together, we brainstormed some ideas. This book-inspired writing is especially beneficial to students who still need structure and a format for their writing. Eventually, open writing and reading reigns during invitation time, and as I mentioned, journal writing is a favorite genre of students.

First Lessons: The Classroom Becomes a Writing Tool

Before any great production, a stage must be set. So it is with my classroom, only I don't set this stage by myself. When school starts, my classroom is barren of bulletin-board and wall displays. In those first weeks of school, my students and I spend a lot of time reading, discovering word and story patterns, predicting story endings, modifying and adapting story versions, acting out story parts, exploring rhyming patterns, and enjoying the rhythms of poetry. From these experiences, the classroom grows stronger in two ways: 1. A rich physical environment of print, meaningful to the children who helped create it, begins to fill the shelves and walls, the baskets and cubbies, and 2. An exciting attitude about literature and writing permeates the atmosphere in the room. Following are more details about the literacy tools that adorn the room and that support children as they work.

An Alphabet Mural & Picture Dictionary

I write the alphabet, upper and lower case, with space in-between the letters, on poster-size paper and hang these sheets with clothespins to form a mural (see photo, next page). In September, I take them down, put them on the tables, and invite children to "visit" all the letters, which means that they draw pictures of objects and people next to any letter they wish. Near the letter *d* are a dinosaur, a dog, a doughnut, a person digging, and a picture of Donnell, a classmate. Before returning these posters to the walls, I label their drawings in standard spelling. And with this, our mural becomes a large, beginning picture dictionary that children refer to throughout the year. Every three months or so, we take them down again, adding additional pictures and vocabulary that we've learned.

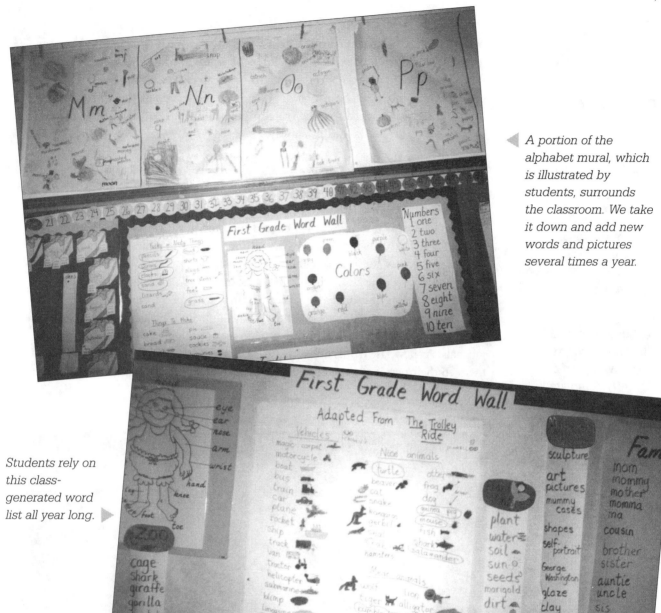

A portion of the alphabet mural, which is illustrated by students, surrounds the classroom. We take it down and add new words and pictures several times a year.

Students rely on this class-generated word list all year long.

The Interactive Word Wall

We dedicate space on the wall for class-generated word lists, which grow during the year. One such list comes from the class reading of *The Trolley Ride*, a predictable, repetitive-pattern book that is a favorite of the class early in the year (see photo). After we read the book several times for enjoyment, the class collaborates to write an adapted version; renditions we've written include "The Raft Ride," "The Limousine Ride," "The Hot-Air Balloon Ride." The list is generated when we brainstorm characters and vehicles for the book. We then

Other Word Lists

Other lists generated from our work and popularly used during journal-writing time are:

Family Words (aunt, uncle, grandmother, grandma, brother, etc.)

Magnetism and Electricity Words (derived from a recently completed unit in science)

Planetarium Words (immediately generated following a field trip)

Halloween Words

Holiday Words

post this list. Children return to the list and others like it throughout the year for ideas or just to find standard spellings of words. I often draw crude illustrations to go alongside the words to help the children differentiate between similarly spelled words. So much of the power and magic of these lists derives from our having worked together to compose them. It is often hard at the end of the year to throw the old lists away.

First-Grade Fast Words

"First-grade fast words" is a term I coined for a process involving the high-frequency sight words that the class and I discover from reading, writing, and language activities (see photo). The words—such as *the, and, some, it,* and *like*—actually don't become "fast words" until I post them on a bulletin board after introducing them. But once displayed, children are expected to spell them correctly in their journals and in all their writing. Midway through the year, I give students a list of these words, and they glue them to the inside covers of their journals. As new fast words are added to the bulletin board, students also add them to their personal copy of the list. Students may suggest words for the list.

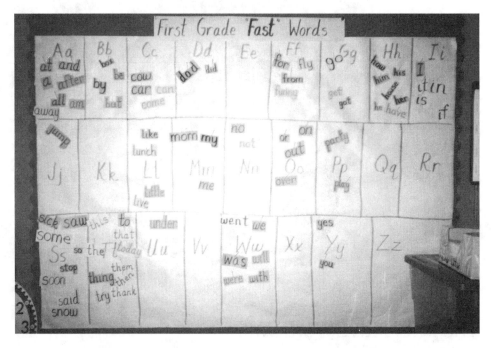

High-frequency first-grade fast words must be spelled correctly during journal writing.

Kicking Off the Journal-Writing Program

Week One

I start journal writing the first week of school, though children don't actually write until the second week. The first week is spent building up the anticipation of journal writing through teacher modeling.

The first day, I brainstorm a list of topics on the chalkboard that I refer to throughout the week. I want writing to be accessible to all students and not limited to only those people who have sensational things to write about, so I share simple stories from home and common classroom situations.

Making the Writing Process Visible

Standing before the class at the overhead projector, I tell a story, interrupting the narration to write a sentence or two or draw a picture. I emphasize beginning sounds, because students in the early stages of writing are often hesitant to put their pencils to paper out of fear that they know so little standard spelling. I deliberately struggle with spelling a couple of words, because I want students to see that my writing does not come to a halt when I have a difficult word to spell. They see me attempt the spelling, say the word aloud so I can listen for the dominant sounds, and then circle the word and go on (see page 50). In the next chapters, I share what these overhead lessons look and sound like.

A Journal Party

My goal in those first weeks is to get everyone writing—from children who write with pictures and strings of random letters to children who already have command of the alphabet. By the end of that first week, children are eagerly anticipating Monday, when they will get their own journals. We kick off the first day of student writing with a party, during which I present each child with a new journal and a special No. 2 pencil. The typical routine then begins in that second week.

Sustaining Motivation: A Lesson From Anne

Throughout the year, I sustain motivation for writing by emphasizing how much I rely on my own journal to remind me of good times. Each week, I spend a few minutes flipping through my collection of entries. I look up at the class and say, "I remember this one. Do you remember when I wrote about running with Todd and Erin down Snake Hill? I'm going to read that again." This technique is powerful, and best of all, I didn't learn it in a graduate course but from a little,

Developmental Levels of Writing

Developed by the Education Department of Western Australia, First Steps give teachers an explicit way of mapping children's progress (in writing, language, reading, and spelling). The developmental phases for writing as defined by First Steps are:

◎ PHASE 1: **Role-Play Writing** Children are beginning to come to terms with a new aspect of language, that of written symbols. They experiment with marks on paper with the intention of communicating a message or emulating adult writing.

◎ PHASE 2: **Experimental Writing** Children are aware that speech can be written down and that written messages remain constant. They understand the left-to-right organization of print and experiment with writing letters and words.

◎ PHASE 3: **Early Writing** Children write about topics that are personally significant. They are beginning to consider audience needs. They have a sense of sentence but may only be able to deal with one or two elements of writing at one time, e.g., spelling but not punctuation.

◎ PHASE 4: **Conventional Writing** Writers are familiar with most aspects of the writing process and are able to select forms to suit different purposes. Their control of structure, punctuation, and spelling may vary according to the complexity of the writing task.

◎ PHASE 5: **Proficient Writing** Writers have developed a personal style of writing and are able to manipulate forms of writing to suit their purposes. They have control over spelling and punctuation. They choose from a large vocabulary, and their writing is cohesive, coherent, and satisfying.

—Education Department of Western Australia. First Steps Writing Developmental Continuum. Portsmouth, NH: Heinemann. 1994. This excerpt used by permission of the publisher.

blond-haired first grader named Anne. Here's how she taught it to me:

Each day, I allow a few students to read aloud a piece of writing from their portfolios. Anne had been anticipating her moment in the spotlight all week. She showed me what she planned to read. It was her journal entry for our trip to the apple orchard. Carefully, she held it in her hands. As I do often at the beginning of the year, I reminded the class that what we place into our portfolio should be our "best stuff," and I asked Anne why she had chosen this piece. I expected her to comment that she'd chosen it for its unusually high amount of writing, its extra-detailed illustrations, its exemplary spelling, or some other effort with writing mechanics. But her response was, "This was my most fun day, and I didn't want to forget about it." With these few words, Anne expressed everything about the value of writing. Preserving a memory of a fall day with her classmates motivated Anne to struggle with her writing mechanics. As she stood before the class and read, she relived the apple orchard and the haunted forest, and her audience did, too. And her teacher was reminded of the importance of forging connections between valued experiences and writing instruction, which can motivate children to want to become writers in our classrooms.

A Close Look at a Journal-Writing Session

I t's 10:05 AM on a Friday in March, and I've just asked my students to get ready for journal writing. As I wheel the overhead projector into position, children open their spirals and copy down today's date at the top of their pages. Excitement is in the air. Earlier this morning, the pet hamster, Chip Chip,

A first grader enjoys 20 minutes of uninterrupted writing.

surprised the class by posting a letter inside her cage insisting that she be served pizza instead of her typical diet of boring bird seed (see illustration). I do not know what the children are more excited about—visions of a hamster rappelling down the cage walls in search of pencil and paper or the thought of their teacher secretively concocting this wild story before school.

Building Anticipation for Journal-Writing Time

I want children to choose their writing topics so that they come to see the value of writing about their own experiences, but for many students, this is difficult, and so I often stage events that serve as optional topics for writing. Chip Chip's letter is one such event. Although journal-writing time occurs later in the morning, I like to get children thinking about topics as soon as they arrive. For children like Leon, Patrick, and Sharie, who are often stumped about topics, I confide my plans to write about Chip Chip. My purpose is twofold: to get them thinking about journal writing ahead of time and to plant the seed that this letter from the classroom pet could be a topic for them.

In time, students discover their own writing topics readily or share news that I encourage them to consider writing about. Some time ago, Amanda bounded into the room and told us about a cellophane-flower craft that she and her Mom made at a Brownies meeting the previous night. "Oh, Amanda, I bet I know what you're going to be writing about in your journal today," I responded.

HAY KIDS,
I SHUR AM
LERNING A LOT.
I LIKE MY NAME.
HOW COME I HAV
TO EAT SEEDS? I
WANT PEETZA.
LUV,
CHIP CHIP

First Goal: Get Every Child Writing

Most children arrive in September excited and eager to share experiences from home or from their ride on the bus. I am always tickled when a student dashes into the room and says, "Oh, Mr. Henry, I already know what I'm going to write about today." But getting them to channel this natural storytelling energy into writing is a process. Writing is a struggle for writers of any age, but for beginning writers, it is even more arduous. The beginning writer must be convinced that she is capable of sharing her adventures via the printed word. From the moment I hand out new journals and pencils, the primary challenge is to get all of the children writing. It is not uncommon for me to see blank journal pages at the end of our writing time in those first weeks. Every time children open their spiral notebooks to write, they must work through phonics, word analysis, punctuation, letter and line spacing, handwriting, and letter identification. Struggling with the mechanics of writing can often derail children from their goal of communicating ideas.

Writing Topics That Matter

Chip Chip's miraculous note offers an irresistible topic. Topics like this are easy to write about—a hamster's pizza plea is extraordinary, funny, and a shared experience, and as such, it helps students who struggle with writing feel immediately at home with their writing topic. Some other staged events and props that have been big hits are:

- photographs from school assemblies or field trips that bring back memories
- requests from the principal asking for help in solving recess problems
- continuing science experiments that offer dramatic change overnight
- notes and photographs from a fictional Farmer Brown who has various troubles with his farm animals
- letters from Bear Bear to his friend Stinky the Skunk (class puppets)
- mysterious appeals to the class from Bob and Martha (box turtles) to settle their arguments regarding the length of earthworms they plan on eating
- fantastic theories that explain a classroom event, such as a hamster's escape from his cage
- predicting an ending to a read-aloud story
- the anticipation of the whole-school Halloween parade
- possible solutions to math story problems

▲ *I write alongside my students, sending the message that writing is relevant and valued by me and other adults.*

Moving Students' Writing Forward by Turning Assumptions About Print Upside Down

The demonstration lessons that I give prior to every journal-writing session provide additional experiences with print that aim to clear up confusions that children may have. Note, however, that sometimes to clear up a student's misconception, you send him into a state of greater confusion. Take the case of Andrea, who confidently ended every line of writing on her page with a period. She noticed after one of my lessons that there were periods missing at the ends of many of my lines. Periods even appeared in the *middle* of some of my lines! Andrea's early understanding of the use of periods was shaken, which showed in the perplexed look on her face and in her writing. After that, she used periods in all sorts of creative ways. I let her find her own way, knowing that with more opportunities to write and more exposure to my demonstration lessons, she would develop a greater understanding of the period's use.

Challenges Are Essential to Learning

Early experiences with print shape children's understandings about spelling and writing. They spend a lot of time watching adults and older siblings model writing and reading activities. Whether it is watching parents pay bills or

listening to a story at a library, children regularly witness the magic and mystery of the alphabet. Children bring these early understandings with them to any writing effort. Any additional information that they receive through experiences at school or home challenge these pre-existing understandings. These challenges are essential for learning, and children need to regularly face them if they are going to refine their understandings of spelling and writing and grow as writers. Jacquelin and Martin Brooks, in their book, *In Search of Understanding: The Case for Constructivist Classrooms* (Association for Supervision and Curriculum Development, 1993), helped me to understand the importance of this challenge:

> Each of us makes sense of our world by synthesizing new experiences into what we have previously come to understand. Often, we encounter an object, an idea, a relationship, or a phenomenon that doesn't quite make sense to us. When confronted with such initially discrepant data or perceptions, we either interpret what we see to conform to our present set of rules for explaining and ordering our world, or we generate a new set of rules that better accounts for what we perceive to be occurring. Either way, our perceptions and rules are constantly engaged in a grand dance that shapes our understandings.

As they write, children engage in this "grand dance," but to extend the metaphor, they are not always light on their feet. Because the mechanics of written language are so new, they trip up a lot. It is hard work, so the payoff must be enjoyment and success. How we respond to young children's early attempts at writing is critical. For those children who have come from classrooms and homes where writing is understood to be developmental and their early attempts have been praised and encouraged, there is little hesitation to begin writing. But many of my students are fearful of the thought of writing for ten minutes, so drawing a picture the entire time is a good beginning step for them. Giving children topics through staged events and continually letting them know their everyday adventures are worthy stories are two ways I make the joyful payoff known.

A Modeling Session: Chronicling Chip Chip the Hamster

The Five-Minute Demonstration

As I mentioned in Chapter 1, I set a simple kitchen cooking timer to provide clear starting and ending times for my modeling. This boundary is important, as it signals to children that for this time, I expect their undivided attention: no pencil sharpening, no talking, no leaving their seats.

Using the tale of Chip Chip as my text, I begin with a review of skills, such as spacing between words and lines, the use of capitals and periods, and spelling. My main emphasis, however, is always my message. I will never be able

to transmit the excitement of writing to my students by making mechanics the emphasis. In time, these mini-reviews move into matters of craft, such as adding more emotion into their writing. My intent as I talk about my writing process is to have children remember this kind of thinking when it's their turn to write. And so I begin:

Mr. Henry: I have been thinking about Chip Chip all morning. Finally, I get to write down what I have been thinking about.

Leon: I knew you were going to write about that hamster, Mr. Henry.

Mr. Henry: You bet I am, Leon. I can't believe he is writing notes now. Now, I know that I tell you this every time, but remember, I'm only going to have a little bit of writing time. And I have so much to say. I may make some mistakes, but don't say anything until after the timer goes off. I just want to get all of my ideas down.

Again, if I'm not sure of any of my spelling, I'll just circle it and worry about it later. I am going to try and remember when I do my writing to get all of my sounds. The beginning sound I hear, the sounds in the middle, and the sound at the end. Right?

[Turning on the projector, I copy at the top of my page the date, 3-7-97, from the chalkboard and then set the timer.]

Scott: You only have five minutes to write, Mr. Henry.

Mr. Henry: That's right, Scott. So, I have to use my time very carefully. And I'm not just going to do boring writing now, either. I'm not just going to write [making my voice monotonic], "There was a note in our hamster tank,"

▲ *Students watch me as I draft a story at the overhead projector during my five minutes of modeling.*

because you guys all know that. I want to write down things that surprise me. Things that make me mad, sad, or glad, or full of wonder. I'm curious about how he got out of the tank to get a marker to write that note. I wish I was standing there when he did it. Okay, here we go.

I know that you guys were surprised, too, when you came in and saw that letter from Chip Chip. I never thought that he could get out of that cage and write us a note. That's what I want to say.

[I move toward the paper on the overhead projector with the intent to begin writing.]

"When we came into school, there was a surprise." *When*. Oh, I know how to spell *ten*.

[I write *ten* on the margin of my journal paper.]

When — ten. They rhyme. They must end the same. But I can tell that *when* starts with a *w*.

[Almost mechanically, I replace the *t* with a *w*. I write out *wen*.]

Hmm. That doesn't look quite right. I'd better circle it.

[Matthew, who is a very good speller, nods in agreement that I have circled my spelling of *when*. Brand'n, who is developmentally behind Matthew, would be content, however, with this phonetic spelling of *when*. I repeat aloud the entire targeted phrase before continuing.]

Mr. Henry: "When we came into school, there was a surprise." *We*, oh, I know that.

Brandon: That's a fast word, Mr. Henry.

Mr. Henry: You are right, Brand'n.

[I write down *we came*.]

I hear three sounds.

[Stretching out *came*, I emphasize the three major sounds: *c aaa mmm*. But I write *cam*.]

Hmmm! It looks like that has the little word *am* inside of it, but it doesn't sound like *am*.

[I underline *am* with the marker. But before I can circle my deliberate misspelling of *came*, a couple of children call out, "There's a quiet *e*!" Many of my students now understand that vowel rule, but some still do not, so I review it for them.]

You mean, by putting a quiet *e* here, I make the *a* say its name?

[Lots of heads nod in agreement. I repeat: "When we came into school, there was a surprise."]

Into. That has two claps. *In* and *to*.

[Hand clapping each syllable helps children both auditorily and visually to make sound discrimination within words.]

[Glancing towards the fast-words chart] There are two fast words in this word. I know them. *Into*. Who remembers what we call two words put into one?

[Many children respond with "compound word." Our text by now looks like this: *Wen we cam into*. At this point in the text, I need to start a new line, and I continue thinking out loud. I remember telling Sam about leaving a space between lines. I've got to remember to do that myself. I reread the whole phrase up to this point.]

Reread Text Often

Anytime that I distract the class away from the message while we attend to spelling or some other area of writing, I always restart by reading aloud what I've written so far, as this models for students what we do as adults when we read or write.

"When we came into school ..." I know about *school*. It's got an *oo* sound in there.

[I slowly write out *school* and underline the *oo* sound.]

"When we came into school . . . today." *d-a-y*

[Everyone chimes in together to spell *day* right after the word *to*.]

Matthew: You need a space, Mr. Henry.

[Timidly, Matthew points between the two words: *to* and *day*. This is taking a big chance for him. He doesn't often call out like this.]

Mr. Henry: Oh, you know what? This is a tricky one. That is a compound word. They go together. It's a word made up of two words: *to* and *day*. I'm glad that you mentioned that. It has two claps. Listen.

[As I say both syllables of the word, I clap them out.]

to day. So, I'm going to keep them together, Matthew.

[I continue, again, by repeating the entire phrase.]

"When we came into school today, there was a surprise."

[The next three words—"... *there was a* ..."—are all written quickly, with references to the fast-words chart. I position a finger between each word on the overhead to remind children about spacing. Finally, I get to the word *surprise*.]

This is kind of tricky. I hear two claps: *sur prise*. Let's do the *sur* part. Can anyone help me? Brand'n, I hear two sounds in *ser—s* and *er*.

[I use two fingers to count out the two major sounds as a visual to Brand'n and the class.]

What should I put?

[Brand'n says this syllable—stretching and emphasizing the two strong phonetic sounds, *s* and *er*. As he says each letter, I copy them onto my transparency. A similar episode follows with the second syllable, *priz*. Another student in the same developmental phase as Brand'n is given similar structure guidelines; this syllable has three sounds: *pr i z*. Jenée, however, misses the *r* sound, and *pis* is dictated onto the paper. My developmental spelling of *serpis* is circled. Again, the circling of this word permits many of my spellers who know the correct spelling to continue without complaint.]

Balancing Storytelling and Instruction

By now, many of my first graders are getting restless. I have pushed the bounds of instruction, so I back away from the overhead and switch into my storytelling mode.

Mr. Henry: The tank looked the same as ever this morning. Chip Chip was all curled up, deep in her pile of bedding. Except, now that I think about it, there was a little pile of cedar chips on the floor leading to the pencil can. And the pencil can was tipped over. Maybe this was part of a trail left by Chip Chip.

Leon: She could have accidentally left those things, Mr. Henry.

Mr. Henry: Maybe. And there were a couple of seed shells on the floor by the can.

Do you think she packed herself a little lunch for her trip to find a marker?
[Trying hard to believe me, many children nod their heads in agreement.]
Let me show you now about this picture.
[Stepping back up to the overhead, I illustrate while I continue talking.]
Here is the tank. Here is the food bowl, and here is her water bottle. And here is all her bedding and stuff. Here was her big pile of bedding. She was in here sleeping when I came in. I think she must have been very tired. And here is this note hanging up. And I just kind of wonder: How … did … she …

Leon: …write that letter?

Mr. Henry: That's right, Leon, How did she *w-r-i-t-e...*

[As I verbally stretch out the sounds for this word, the class joins in with me to help me identify the strong phonetic sounds *rit.* I'm going to circle *that.* The final two words in this sentence, *that* and *letter,* are written down with no input from the class. As I write, I recite them, emphasizing their dominant consonant blends. Now I back away from the overhead.]

How did she do that! Now, I've seen people when they climb down mountains. They have a rope that they tie somewhere, and then they lean backwards while holding onto the rope and take big jumps while holding onto the rope like this.

[As I role-play this scene for the kids, I once again have their full attention. I hear shouts of "Oh, I've seen that kind on TV before" and "I've done that before."]

Tips on Storytelling

From the very start of the year, I refer to fiction as stories that are "made-up" and nonfiction as "not made-up stories." When children tell stories about the lunchroom or tales from home at journal-writing time, I continually ask the class, "Is the story fiction or nonfiction? How do you know?" so they learn the distinction between these genres.

For staged events that generate writing topics, I like to have an object for the children to focus on. Letters work very well. In the course of the year, I stage letters from Chip Chip, Bob, and other class pets; from Stinky, Bear Bear, and other class puppets; from the principal and teachers; and from former students.

Most of the modeling that I do in front of the children is not from staged experiences. As I've said, stories from my personal life thrill the children. I usually select a topic and generate ideas ad lib while standing at the overhead projector during modeling time. When I have trouble thinking of a topic or generating ideas, that's okay. I tell students about it. I want them to see my struggle and observe how I handle it. I know that they will need to solve similar problems.

Well, I wonder if Chip Chip was doing that.

[Instantly, there are squeals of delight as children visualize a hamster rappelling down a mountain. I continue to talk and write.]

I think I know why she has so much of that bedding piled up in the corner of her cage. Not only does it make a soft bed, but also she can hide stuff in there. She must be hiding all of that equipment that she needs to get down from her cage. I bet underneath all that bedding there are a rope and special boots that she wears. Maybe she has an extra pen in there for writing letters.

[The final sentence—"Maybe she hides things under her bed"—is very phonetic. Sensing an urgency to move on, I finish the modeling by taking less input from the children.]

That's what I'm going to write. "Maybe she hides things under her bed." *May* rhymes with *day*. I'm just going to change the *d* to an *m*. *Maybe b e she* [I automatically write down *she*] *hides*—I'm going to need some help with *hides*.

[Stretching out the major sounds, we end up with *hids*. Before I can continue, one of my better spellers suggests that I circle this spelling. For my emergent spellers who helped me write down *hids*, circling this word again would not be necessary. The major sounds of this word are obvious, and they are all accounted for in this spelling.]

"Maybe she hids things…"

[The word *things* is separated into three main parts: *th ing s*. These are easy for the children, and I receive instant answers from the class. Since the very beginning of journal writing back in the fall, the sound of *ing* has always been pronounced as one sound.]

"Maybe she hides things under her bed."

Matthew: [shouts out] *Under* is one of our fast words.

Mr. Henry: Thanks, Matthew.

[I'm glad to hear this from Matthew, as he rarely checks the fast-word charts for spelling help. *Under* is quickly written out, pausing between syllables. Again, starting from the beginning of this sentence, I reread up to the next work spot.] "Maybe she hides things under her bed."

[As *her* and *bed* are written down—RING!—the timer sounds. The kids offer to give me more time when I express disappointment that journal time for me is over.]

After the Bell Rings: A Few Minutes to Model Proofreading

When the bell rings, that is my cue to wrap up the demonstration lesson with rereading that will hit home some final points. This is the time when the children and I review what I have written and attend to words that I have circled. This is also a time to resolve punctuation and other writing issues that I have deliberately created. In this example, I spend some time attending to words in the text that were circled. Here is how it might go:

Farewell to Jake the Snake

Throughout the year, I purposely choose writing topics generated from shared class experiences that any student could write about. The best way to gauge whether the topic will inspire students is to think about the degree of students' emotional involvement in the topic. One of my most successful topics was a garter snake with whom my children had fallen in love.

On a Friday morning early in September, I informed the class that I had chosen my topic while driving to school. "I'm a little excited and a little sad about today," I said. A little garter snake had been a visiting pet, and all week long, the children had enjoyed observing him in the aquarium and solving Jake the Snake math problems. This was Jake's last day. "I want to write about Jake. I'm going to miss him. Later this year, when the snow is on the ground and Jake is hibernating in the ground, I want to be able to turn back to my journal and remember him." The children expressed their wishes to write about their time with Jake. We talked about Jake. Some students were concerned that his family won't remember Jake. Others anticipated the details of Jake's welcome-home party. During sharing time, children stood in line "tank-side" to read their parting entry to Jake.

When we steer children toward topics with which they have emotional connections, the rest takes care of itself.

Mr. Henry: I'm going to read this over and see if I can fix any of these words that are circled. *Wen we cam to school today there was a serpis. How did she rit that letter? Maybe she hids things under her bed.*

By focusing the discussion on advanced-spelling rules, I address the needs of many students. I read the first sentence just as it was dictated. On the last sentence—"*Maybe she hids things under her bed*"—I pronounce the word *hides* just as it is spelled (*hids*), and immediately this causes problems with the meaning. Someone suggests that a quiet *e* is missing, so I write the correct spelling above the circled one. This clues children in to other circled words—*cam, serpis*, and *rit*—and they announce that they are all missing final *e*'s.

The missing *w* in *write* is not noticed, and I decide not to pursue it. Finally, a discussion ensues about the different ways that we can make the *er* sound. In our guided-writing lessons, the *er* sound has always been written as *e r*. Briefly, we talk about how *or, ur, ir, ar*, as well as *er* can all at times make the *er* sound. A few examples are given, and *serpise* is changed to *surprise*.

Leon, an emergent reader and writer, includes periods at the end of every line of his writing. I am pleased that he is developing an awareness of punctuation. He notices, however, that many of my lines do not have periods at the end, and he is confident enough in this open session to raise this point in the class discussion. To help illustrate the function of periods, I temporarily place periods at the end of every line and quickly read the new journal entry, stopping at every period.

When we came into.
school today there was a.
surprise. How did she rite.
that letter? Maybe she hides.
things under her bed.

My first graders chuckle at the nonsense I've made. I invite them to correct it, and they do. Leon benefits from his peers' insights, though he will need more modeling sessions like this before punctuation clicks for him.

The focus of this lesson was on stretching out words to hear all the beginning, middle, and ending sounds. There was a heavy emphasis on writing mechanics. Tomorrow, I may focus the session on developing a writer's voice by adding more opinion to my writing. I continually strike a balance between the art and the craft of writing.

Student Writing Time: 15 Minutes

As I wheel the overhead projector away, my students make final preparations to write in their journals.

"Pencils up!" I announce. With this command, conversations quiet and everyone raises pencils high in the air.

"Begin!" I set the timer to 15 minutes. Many of my writers begin immediately, and many will write about Chip Chip. A few others need more time to mull over their topics. I want them immersed in the writing as quickly as possible. I want them to learn not to agonize over writing decisions, because they can always be reworked. Children decide on topics, on whether to continue writing from a previous day or to start fresh with a new idea. They decide which letters make beginning, middle, and ending sounds, and when to use punctuation. And with these decisions come revisions, new ideas, and ultimately, a greater understanding of their topics.

I usually give the class five minutes of writing time before I begin to make my rounds. This morning, I notice that Donnell, who is new to the class and who sits opposite Sam, is so frustrated about his spelling that he is asking Sam for confirmation on every word, keeping Sam from writing. First, I comment on how happy I am that he is writing about his swimming lessons. Then, I ask Donnell which words he is having trouble spelling. I model circling those words for now and encourage him to continue on with his ideas.

As students settle into their writing, I tell them how pleased I am to see that so many are remembering to leave spaces between their lines so that there is room to edit spelling mistakes later. Brittany, who in the past has left huge margins on both sides of her pages and consequently was writing only two or three words on a line, has remembered to start at the faint red line on the left of her notebook page. I praise her in a stage whisper so that the entire class is

reminded to pay attention to their margins.

Reading and writing noises fill the room. Some children are busy stretching out sounds and syllables of words, while others reread writing in pursuit of new thoughts. Sam proudly shares why he is taking the circle off of the word *bunch*. "When I was writing *brunch*, I said *brunch*. I was thinking what it rhymes with, and I said *lunch*, and I was looking for *lunch*. And I looked up there [he points to the day schedule on the chalkboard, which includes the correct spelling] and took the *l* away."

▲ *A first grade journal writer is hard at work.*

Motivating Students as They Write

On a typical journal-writing day, I move around the class about one-and-a-half times, starting my rounds at a different table each session. The purpose of my travels is to motivate by validating children's efforts. Sitting beside them or leaning over their shoulder, I read their work aloud in a whisper and give them feedback.

During earlier days with journal writing, I used this time to help students spell or fix their spelling, sending the unintended message that writing mechanics is what I value the most. But after reading Frank Smith's *Joining the Literacy Club* (Heinemann, 1988), I've realized that "emphasis on the suppression of errors results in the suppression of writing." Children write more and take more chances in their writing when I encourage the message.

Encouraging a Writer of Few Words

Stooping down beside Scott, I say, "Let's see what Scott is writing about today."

Scott is a pretty good writer. He looks forward to journal writing. He always seems to have a topic to write about, and he's eager to share his writing when he is finished. His invented spelling is phonetic and easy to read. He doesn't produce as much writing as I think he probably could, however.

"Oh, you are going to tell me about that Crunch game. I'm glad they won, Scott. Did you go to the game?"

"Yes, with my Dad. Hector Marinaro got the winning goal. He is my favorite player."

"I'm glad you are writing about soccer, Scott. I hope the Crunch can make it to the playoffs. When I come back around, maybe I'll find out even more about the game." I want Scott to think, "Wow, Mr. Henry was really interested in what I have to say. He is going to be back to find out more."

Reaching a Tentative Writer

I head over to Neal, a new student. He is a little more tentative in his writing than Scott. After nine minutes, he has written only one sentence.

"Neal, I'm glad that you are writing about moving into your new home. That has to be very exciting. Will you be sharing a room with your brother?"

"No, I will have my own room. My birthday is coming up, and we're going to get a basketball hoop."

"Wow, Neal, you have so many exciting things to write about. I'll come back in a little bit and see what else you put down." I make a note to check back with Neal.

Striking a Deal With a Writer Stymied by Spelling

It is difficult for some children to keep writing when they know there are misspelled words on their paper, whether they circle the words or not. Amanda is one of those students, so she and I have a deal. She will write and circle misspelled words if I will help her to fix them when I get to her during my walk-around.

Amanda waits patiently while I carefully read the first page of her writing.

"Amanda, you're going on an airplane all by yourself?"

"I need help, Mr. Henry, with *flowergirl.*"

"Well, it is actually two separate words, Amanda. *Flower* and *girl.* Let us do the first one. *Flower.* It has two claps. *Flow* and *er.*" On the margin of her notebook, I write *cow.* "*Flow* rhymes with *cow.*" Amanda crosses off the *c* and puts an *f* in its place. I help her pronounce the new word part, *fow.* She immediately knows to add an *l.* "You know how to make the *er* sound." She needs little help with the second word—*girl.*

Amanda adds, "Also, *cousin* I need help with."

"Oh, well, you know where to find the word *cousin.* It is right on the family chart. Do you see it, Amanda?" Pointing to the Family Words chart posted on the bulletin board, I leave Amanda to finish copying this word into her journal.

Brittany eagerly awaits my visit with her. She hides her journal from me and then proceeds to read to me. With delight, she reveals her thoughts about the real Chip Chip letter writer.

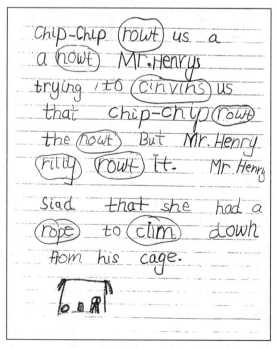

▲ *Brittany's journal entry, written after my modeled writing about Chip Chip the hamster.*

▲ *Students share journal stories with friends.*

The Final Stage: Sharing Time

The timer's bell goes off. The noise level increases. While some children continue to write or illustrate, others talk or read their work with classmates.

Since I have already interacted with everyone, I encourage children to share with one another rather than me. Not that they're discriminating about their audience—it's not uncommon to see children standing before Chip Chip's and Bob the turtle's tanks, reading aloud their writing. This is especially true when the pets are the subject of the journal entries. (See box on page 37, *Farewell to Jake the Snake*) I like to joke with students, telling them that I saw Chip Chip move some of the cedar chips so that she might hear them read better. Rereading leads to rewriting and editing. I remember being frustrated over my attempts to get first graders to read back over their work to check for mistakes. No matter how often I tried, I could not get them to edit their writing. I did find, however, that my students love to share their adventures with classmates when writing time is over. As they circulate around the classroom reading to friends, I require them to travel with a pencil in hand. When omitted words and letters in the rereading are discovered, it is not uncommon to see them pause and edit.

The class pets are favorite "classmates" with whom kids share journal entries.
▼

41

Meeting the Needs of My Students

Even though everyone has had a chance to read to me, a few students insist on capturing my attention at sharing time. Certain children, perhaps especially those who are new to the class, need the compassionate ear of a teacher to listen to their concerns. Of course, I'm always available.

Emily reads me a three-page entry describing a scary bicycle accident that happened the day before. "Emily, this is a good example of writing that is sure not boring. I am sure glad that you are okay. That had to be very scary."

Next, Natasha, who is also very new to the class and does not quite know all of her sounds and letters, reads about seeing Amanda at the roller rink. Amanda, sitting within earshot, responds with big smiles.

Donnell reads aloud his vignette about swimming lessons at Thornton Park. Children sitting close enough to hear Donnell now buzz with their own Thornton Park stories.

For Donnell and Natasha, struggling readers and writers, sharing has been a successful experience, helping them to view themselves as writers. I know they will be eager to share again. And for Amanda and others, hearing classmates' stories evoked memories of swimming, Thornton Park, and reinforced the idea that writing can make people feel happy, nostalgic, and all sorts of emotions.

All students have stories to tell. And they will tell them if they have active listeners to hear them. Connecting these personal stories to direct writing instruction provides for powerful learning.

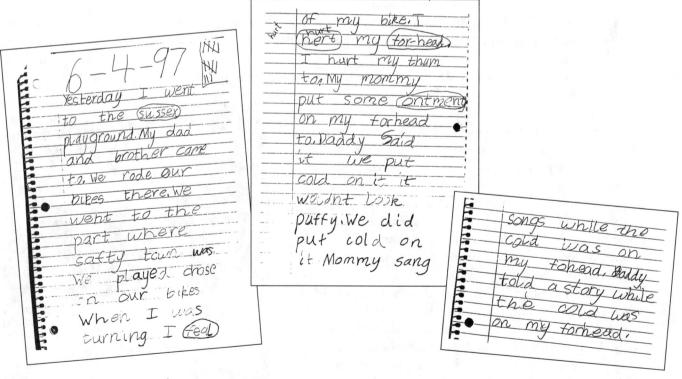

Journal writing preserves memories and helps children work through difficult events.

Basic-Skill Instruction and the Journal

As I learned from Anne, it's the memories of trips to the zoo, sleep overs with friends, and jumping in fall-leaf piles that children value. The personal-writing journal is a place for students to write about what means the most to them. But mastering the basic skills of writing is also necessary. And because the personal-writing journal is such a great vehicle for authentic writing, it offers opportunities for both individual and whole-class instruction in reading and writing skills. Chip Chip and the demonstration lesson gave a glimpse of this.

Feedback from peers is a powerful motivator for writers.

In this chapter, I share strategies to use during improvised and planned skill instruction. I explain how I teach spelling through two whole-class lessons students and I call "The Little-Paper Spelling Lesson" and "Chalkboarding Circled Words." And because powerful instruction often takes place following journal writing—when children excitedly share their work—I share how I use these teachable moments to conduct "Lesson-in-the-Margin."

I focus on spelling instruction, sharing what's worked for me, and giving you strategies that go beyond the traditional weekly spelling test, and are useful when reporting to parents.

Lesson-in-the-Margin: Hotdogday

Like most teachers, my direct writing-skill instruction falls into two basic categories: 1. weekly, preplanned lessons that take place outside of our regular 30-minute journal-writing sessions, and 2. impromptu, informal lessons that spring up regularly within the writing period. First, here's a look at an impromptu lesson:

A few minutes into journal writing, I spotted Leah smiling and beckoning me with her hand. She pointed to a circled word. "Mr. Henry, I think I figured out a compound word that has three words in it—*hotdogday.*" Bending down beside her, I took out my pencil and began a lesson-in-the-margin about compound words.

Andrea consults her ring words to confirm a spelling.

▲ *I lead a lesson-in-the-margin with a student.*

As writing teachers, we must seek out these unplanned, teachable moments that are a part of every teaching day, for they are often the most "natural" powerful teaching we conduct. Why? When the child initiates the lesson, it is clearly fulfilling the child's need, so the child is more likely to absorb the information.

To make the most of these moments, I always ask myself the same two questions: What does the child know? and How can I connect what she knows about words to what she does not know, and teach a strategy along the way? Often, spelling issues arise: "How do you spell *dinosaur*?" or "Does *getting* have two *t*'s or one?" I like to see a child's first attempt. That tells me so much more of what he knows and gives me a starting point for instruction.

While Leah inspired a lesson-in-the-margin by showing me something she had discovered on her own, it is more often the case that a lesson-in-the-margin emerges when a student reads aloud to a friend. This is when children first become aware of the problems in their writing—their oration stumbles or stops when meaning has faltered or when they hit a spelling glitch. They have not yet developed the skill of self-editing—stopping during drafting and rereading text to make sure that it flows fluently and that it makes sense to the reader. Young writers learn this through experience.

When the child reads her work to me, I look for ways to foster self-editing skills. I ask, "What can we do to make this easier for you and me to read?" And then I let the child tell me or work it out by herself.

Picking Your Lessons

Often, on any page of a student journal, there are a multitude of lessons to tackle. I don't try to address them all. There isn't the time to do so, and if I pointed out every spelling and grammatical mistake to the child, I would crush his enthusiasm. Between journal writing and the daily invitation or independent-writing times, I know that there will be many opportunities for my students to construct writing knowledge with and without my help. So, I concentrate first on the skill questions the children have. I want to meet their needs. After considering the children's level of reading and writing, I may move into other lessons. I may not choose to spend time teaching higher-level concepts, such as the difference between the use of homonyms *their* and *there*, when the child is confusing the consonant digraphs *sh* and *ch*. These lessons-in-the-margin are quick, sometimes lasting no more than a few seconds. Here's a look at a few of them:

Connecting to Better-Known Fast Words

cor for *card*

Mr. Henry: Matteo, do you remember this word, for?

Matteo: *For. f-o-r*

Mr. Henry: Good! What if I take off the *f* and put in a *c*?

Matteo: *Cor. c-o-r*

Mr. Henry: [pointing now to his text] You didn't want to say *cor* right here. How can we change it to *card*? Do you remember this fast word?

Matteo: [turning over his journal cover to reveal the student copy of first-grade fast words and pointing to the word *car*] *Car. c a r*

Mr. Henry: How can we change it to *card*?

Matteo: Put a *d* at the end.

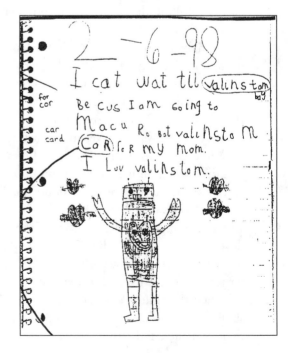

Zeroing in on Unknown Elements

birtday for *birthday*

Mr. Henry: Anna, what part of this word are you not sure about?

Anna: The first clap [syllable].

Mr. Henry: I hear three big sounds. [As I say each major sound—*b er th*—I draw three empty underline marks.] You got the first sound, didn't you? [I fill in the first space with a *b*.] Do you remember, Anna, all the different ways that we can make the *er* sound? [As she lists all the vowel-*r* combinations, I write them down.] You did a great job picking the right one. [I write *ir* in the next blank.]

Anna: I think a *th* goes here [she points to the last space].

> 1-22-98
> I am going to have my (birtday) party in April. I think that will be fun.
>
> b ir th day
>
> er
> ir
> ur
> or
> ar

Selected Lessons in Phonics

sowed for *should*   *hiede* for *hide*

Mr. Henry: Lauren, let's work on two of your words for now. You pick them.

Lauren: *Should* and *hide* [she points and checks them off in her journal as she tells me].

Mr. Henry: Let's work on *should*. [At the bottom of her journal, I lightly write *see* and *she* next to each other.] You know these two words, don't you?

Lauren: [pointing to each] *See* and *she*.

Mr. Henry: Which one of these words starts the same as *should*?

Lauren: [thinking for only a second] *She*.

Mr. Henry: Good job, Lauren. [Rather then go into all of the possible *ow* sounds and *ould* word chunks that form this word, I write out the remainder of the word.]

Lauren, I like how you tried this word *hide*. It shows me that you know a lot about words. [I write down the two spellings: *hied* and *hide*.] Lauren, which one of these looks like the word *hide*?

Lauren: [pointing to the correct one—*hide*] This one.

Mr. Henry: Good work. [And we circle it. Had she not recognized it, I would have told her.]

> 2-23-98
> I made some clay art. I made a cat. And a (gerrafa). My Dad loves (gerrafas) So my Mom side we (sowed) (hiede) It.
>
> hied
> (hide)
>
> should
>
> see
> she

Common rimes

A rime is a vowel pattern in a syllable. It's also called a *chunk* or a common spelling pattern. Here are some my students get a lot of mileage out of:

sh**e**
c**ar**
k**eep**
d**ay**
c**at**
sch**ool**
out
c**ow**
m**y**
for

Circled Words and First-Grade Fast Words

"The ability to spell easily and automatically enables us to become more effective writers. The less energy and thought we have to put into thinking about spelling, the more thought we can put into what is said…. Learning to spell is not learning lists of words. It is a developmental process of learning to apply different strategies appropriately, so that we can spell correctly all the words we write."[2] Circled words and first-grade fast words are writing tools that enhance the developmental processes of learning to spell. They provide me with beginning points for strategy instruction in spelling and help children view spelling as a thinking process, not a rote "memorization hoop" they must jump through.

Let's take a look at both circled words and first-grade fast words.

Introducing First-Grade Fast Words

First-grade fast words comprise an ever-growing, carefully selected list of high-frequency sight words that are discovered and developed individually in class. The list is maintained on a bulletin board and in the front inside cover of every student's journal.

My students and I start to develop first-grade fast words the first week of school. Sitting with the big book *Time for a Rhyme*, a collection of nursery rhymes that the class and I have read many times, I lead the class in the discovery of how often the word *the* shows up in these poems. On a chalkboard next to the reading easel, a volunteer tallies every time *the* appears. I act amazed with each new sighting, and before long, children are hurriedly scanning the text for new appearances each time we turn the page. When a student notices two *the*'s on the cover of *The Field Beyond the Outfield* by Mark Teague, which is on the nearby book stand, the search for *the* now extends into every corner of the classroom. We jokingly refer to this day as National THE DAY.

"Do you think there are any other words in this book that are so popular?" I ask. A similar scene ensues for the words *and* and *to*. Up until now, the front bulletin board has remained empty except for the heading First Grade Fast Words and the alphabet, which I've printed in large letters and spaced out evenly in three rows. Now, with a black marker and a piece of green construction paper, I write out in inch-tall letters the three words discovered during shared reading: *the, and, to*. I cut out each word in its configured shape and post it on the bulletin board next to its initial letter.

---

2. *First Steps Spelling Continuum*, page 15.

We enjoy poetry in a shared reading session.

Mr. Henry: Why do you think we call these words *first-grade fast words*?

Lauren: We can say them fast?

Mr. Henry: Let's try them and see. [I lead the class in reciting these single-syllable words in rapid succession.] You guys are right. I can say them fast. But there is another reason why we can call them *fast words*. Now whenever we see them in a book or write them in our journals, we don't have to spend a lot of time trying to figure them out, because we can just look up and see them.

Throughout the year, I make reference to this growing list of fast words in my journal-writing modeling, during reading groups, when we're looking at displays in the hallways, and in other shared-reading and -writing adventures. I teach my class the expectation that is hinged on each of these words: When a word becomes a first-grade fast word, students should not circle it or spell it phonetically. Whenever they use the word now, I expect them to spell it correctly. I tell them that time out for decoding will no longer have to be taken for these words; it is a known sight word that should automatically be written or read.

Well, in reality it doesn't always work that way. Children will not always spell and read a new word correctly just because we have posted it on a bulletin board. But an important distinction between this category of high-frequency words and the remaining body of words has been created.

Adding to the Fast-Words List

The fast-words list develops all year long. We often come across new fast words to add during shared-writing and -reading sessions. Sometimes, students will nominate a fast word they've come across in their own reading and writing. Often, my decision to include a word as a first-grade fast word is based on its high utility for later lessons. For example, the words *car, day, school, keep, out, her,* and *my* are chosen not just because of the numerous rimes associated with these words but because of dominant phonemic elements found within them. For example, when students hit a challenging word such as *starting, farmer,* or *partner,* I want them to be able to call upon the fast word *car,* with its *ar* sound and similar spelling, to help them decode. To help a student who is stumped by an unfamiliar word, I ask, "What do you already know about this word? Are there letters, blends, digraphs, rimes, small words, prefixes, suffixes, and other word chunks contained within this word that can help you?"

Making and Breaking Words

By midyear, my students can anticipate my response when they ask me how to spell or read an unknown word. If the unknown word is from a book, I might copy the word onto a small chalkboard. Then I'll ask them, "What do you know about this word?" As they tell me what they notice—for example, the beginning *s,* the *er* sound made from *ur,* the fast word *at* buried within the word, or maybe the *e* sound made from *ee*—I underline each separate part with chalk. In so doing, a long, intimidating word becomes a more approachable series of underlined sections.

Then, I'll say, "Look, you know every part of this word. Put it together now, and tell me what it is." Often, even if the child cannot get all of the parts of the word, enough elements are familiar that the word becomes recognizable, especially when reread in context. The highly effective Reading Recovery Program includes as a part of its daily regimen the similar use of magnetic letters to work on making and breaking words. With this method, children become less intimidated by unknown words. They have more strategies and are more willing to make attempts at words. I tell them that I'm not always going to be next to them to help them when they are reading. Eventually, I want them to learn to ask themselves the question "What do I know?"

Circled Words

Students are often aware of misspelled words in their writing. This is good. The downside, though, is that students will stall or stop their writing when they want to use a word they're not sure how to spell. As I've said, I want to see students writing more than I want to see perfect spelling at the drafting stage, so I lean on a technique that keeps correct spelling "in a holding pattern" until students finish their writing This is accomplished by asking students to circle the words whose spelling they're unsure of. This is a way

for the young writer to signal to me that he still has reasonable doubts about his spelling. This technique is usually successful in getting students to continue on with their writing. Every student knows that we will deal with these needs later.

Circled Words Generate Lessons

When I read my students' work, I try to figure out why they have circled a word, which part of the word they're uncertain of. Rarely is the student making a total guess. Children are sure of much of their spelling. Focusing on that uncertain element provides me with opportunities for teaching and learning. The unsure element is like a laser beam letting me know which words or word parts to teach. Going into the lesson, I know my students are interested in these words. This is very different than the feeling I used to get when I conducted lessons using the lists of isolated vocabulary words in formal spelling programs.

The direct instruction that is prompted by these circled words results in either a lesson-in-the-margin or a formal lesson that takes place outside of the journal-writing time, such as a chalkboard spelling lesson or a little-paper spelling lesson.

Little-Paper Spelling Lesson

The little-paper spelling lesson is a whole-class, interactive lesson that is popular with the students. I am not really sure why they like it so much. It is probably one of my more powerful lessons, because the children have a personal interest in the outcome. The lesson is not performed every day. Instead, we do this weekly, or if there are a lot of other things going on, once every other week.

The announcement of the lesson is greeted with a cheer. The children automatically know to clear their desks. Quarter sheets of scrap paper ripped in front of the children are passed to each child. By midpoint in the year, I no longer have to announce to everyone to place his or her name and date on the paper. The lesson focuses on a single word that I have chosen. It is a word that I see spelled incorrectly in many of the children's journals. These are usually high-frequency words that I know the children are using in their speech, seeing in their reading, and using in their writing. I select the words with various goals in mind:

◎ to review dominant phonemes, such as those found in *town, going, keep, lunch,* or *went*

◎ to reinforce some structural elements that are common in words, such as the *ar* sound in *party* and *car;* the consonant blends and digraphs found in *thank, from, lunch;* or the *ay* sound found in *today* and *play*

◎ to reinforce some spellings of words that need to be learned, such as *said, saw, little,* or *was*

◎ to work with syllables in intimidating, "long" words, such as *yesterday, morning, finished*

A Little-Paper Spelling Lesson in Action

In this lesson, I work with the word *after*. This is a word that is highly phonetic. It has two syllables, although in my class, we say that it has two claps: *af* (clap) *ter* (clap). It is a sight word that I want the children aware of, and following the lesson, it's destined for our fast-words chart. I know that many of my students already know how to spell this word, and they will be excited to exhibit this knowledge. But being successful here means more than just spelling a word correctly. Success will mean defending their understandings of spelling before their peers. For those students who cannot yet spell *after* correctly, the word is familiar enough to them that they will eagerly attempt it.

Prior to announcing the word, I glance around the class. The children are well aware by January of the literary-rich surroundings in the class and will make a sporting attempt to find today's word on posted poems, stories, lists, and murals in an effort to solve today's word problem. The word *after*, however, is not visible. (If it was, I'd cover it up.)

When I announce the word, students get busy writing what they think is the correct spelling on a piece of paper. I hear some murmuring of "This is an easy one" or "I know this one." Soon, I hear the rustle of papers flipped over—the signal that students are done and ready to proceed. I pick up their papers, shuffle them in front of the class, and write each version of the word in a list form on the chalkboard, just as the children wrote them. Today, we have seven different versions. I number the list:

1. afder
2. aftre
3. afry
4. after
5. afther
6. afbr
7. afler

Often, our list is much longer. Repeat spellings are listed only once on the board. I ask if everyone can locate their spelling on the list. Today, Matteo is unable to do so and raises his hand. Since I have already collected all the papers, I ask Matteo to approach me, and I show him his paper. After a few glances up and down from his paper to the board, he finds the word with a smile. Many of the children are proud of their spelling and want to share it with classmates. With all of the spellings listed on the board, some of the children who previously wrote the word incorrectly on their slips of paper are now able to recognize the corrected spelling on the list.

Winnowing the Possibilities

Now begins a process of narrowing down the spellings to the correct standard spelling. Since most of the children will see their spelling attempt crossed out in full view of the class, I downplay whose version is whose. We begin by noticing the similarities of all the entries. Children point out that in all the spellings, there are an *a*, *f*, and *r* and notice that many of the spellings contain *e* and *t*.

Someone notices that all of the spellings begin with an *af*.

"Does anyone see a spelling of *after* that you just know cannot be correct?" I ask. Hands shoot into the air. This is what the children have been waiting for. The focus of the lesson now turns to a critical study of words. Andrea responds, "I think we should cross out number six, *afbr*. That word has a *b* in it, and I don't hear a *b* when I say *after*."

Inviting Students to Make a Case

My students' mission is to build a case to convince their classmates of why a version on the list should be crossed out. Their reason must be convincing, because for every entry on the list, there is at least one student in the class who believes it is the correct spelling. I serve as a moderator to make sure that the other children understand the students' arguments. "Andrea feels that we should strike out number six—*afbr*—because when she says the word slowly, she doesn't hear a *b* in there at all. Let's say it slowly again, and listen to see if we hear a *b* sound."

We stretch the word out slowly, listening for every sound. "Okay, do you agree that we should cross out number six, because there is not suppose to be a *b* in there?" I ask.

I hear a chorus of yes's and cross out number six. Anyone who remains unconvinced is encouraged to call out or signal me somehow. When that's the case, I would have said, "Andrea, I can't cross this word out yet. You may be correct, but you haven't convinced the whole class that you are right." At that point, another student may succeed in debunking number six with a different argument that convinces everyone. This is where the lesson is made challenging for the whole class. For even though a student may know the correct spelling of the target word, being articulate enough to convince classmates of your understandings about spelling rules is not always easy.

Giving Weaker Spellers a Chance to Shine

The lesson continues. Early in the lesson, when the list has many obvious misspellings, I choose students at the early stages of the spelling development continuum to make their cases for specific words to be struck out. Later, when the list is narrowed down to words with more sophisticated spelling-rule differences, these students are less likely to contribute.

My role throughout is critical. I use this stage to extend the lesson and make connections from students' understandings about spelling to the unknown. Language and pronunciation issues often arise. For example, when number one on the list, *afder*, is analyzed by the class, we note the small differentiation in sounds between *after* and *afder* before striking it from the list. Many students had campaigned for *afder* as the correct spelling, so I make a point of marveling at how close in sound it is.

Marquez doesn't try to cite a spelling rule when he suggests number three be stricken from the list. Instead, he hopes to convince the class with his pronunciation of this fictional new word: "Number three can't be *after*, because it would say *afree*."

"Marquez remembers how we have learned that many words, such as *funny*,

party, and *Ashley*, have two claps or more and also end with a *y*. The *y* makes them have an *ee* sound at the end. What about other words that have *y*'s at the end?" On the chalkboard, I write *by, my, shy, sky, why.* "Let's say these words together. What sound is at the end of all these words?" The class notes the long *i* sound. Similarly, we write *may, play, today,* and *away,* and note the *ay* sound. In conclusion, "We know a lot about words that end with *y*. Does it sound like *after* should end with a *y*?" The vote to reject *afry* is simple, and we proceed on. I get similar teaching mileage out of *afbr, afther,* and *afler,* and our list now looks like this:

> 1. ~~afder~~
> 2. aftre
> 3. ~~afry~~
> 4. after
> 5. ~~afther~~
> 6. ~~afbr~~
> 7. ~~afler~~

The Suspense Builds

When we get to the final two words, there is a little more tension in the class, as most of the children have taken sides with these two words. "Let's look at these last two spellings, *aftre* and *after.*" I am surprised that *aftre* has survived this long. The *er* sound is common to my class, but we continue. Arguments for both words are made. Stubbornness prevails, and an agreement is not made. So that we don't debate well beyond when the school buses leave, I locate the word in a book and show it to students. *After* is found in the book *Bill and Pete* by Tomie dePaola.

When it is all over, I commend the class. "You all did a very good job today. Look at all of the spellings of *after*. All of them are very close to the correct way that we spell it. I would be a little worried if I saw that someone had tried to spell it [I take a piece of chalk and write some letters randomly on the board] like this— *bzlro*." We end the lesson with the children copying *after* onto their individual first-grade fast-words charts, while I add the word to our whole-class chart.

Chalkboarding Circled Words

Chalkboarding circled words is another spelling lesson that often follows the journal-writing period. After distributing individual student chalkboards and chalk, I ask, "Does anyone have a circled word in their journal from today's writing that they would like help with?" Usually, every hand in the class goes up. With my class grouped around five tables, I select one student from each table, often choosing students at different developmental spelling levels.

Students, in turn, announce the word and read the journal text that contains the circled word. I copy the word on the chalkboard just as the student spelled it.

"What part of this spelling are you not sure about?" I ask. Then I underline whichever letters, word chunks, or syllables the child states.

Now it is time for the rest of the class to participate. Just as the little paper spelling lesson requires each child to make a prediction, I want each child to have a personal stake in this lesson, and so instruct the class to help figure out how to spell this word by writing it on their little chalkboards. After I have circulated around the classroom, I return to the chalkboard, and the lesson begins. Because every child has a circled word, I keep each word lesson brief. I want to get to as many children as I can in this 20–25-minute session. I conduct these lessons one or two times a week.

A Chalkboard Spelling Lesson

Lucas was the first chosen to receive help. Lucas was an average reader, and he felt honored to be selected first. He read aloud from his journal: "I'm going to my Daddy's apartment." He shared with the class his attempted spelling of the word *apartment*, and I wrote it on the chalkboard: *uportmit*. "What part of this spelling are you unsure about?" I asked.

"I am not sure of the *o-r*. It might be something else." I tell the class, "Lucas needs some help with *apartment*. He knows that *o-r* usually makes the *or* sound that we hear in the fast word *for*." I write *for* close to Lucas's spelling, underlining

▲ Classmates help one another during a chalkboard spelling lesson.

the *or*. "But he is thinking that maybe in this word, the *o-r* doesn't make that sound. Lucas did a good job of remembering that *apartment* has three claps [syllables]: *a part ment*. And so, that means that there must be at least three vowels." I point to each of Lucas's vowels. "So, see if you can help Lucas."

Students get to work, writing on their chalkboards. A few children would have been content with Lucas's version, but my preamble causes them to take a closer look. After moving around the class for a while, I see that most people have finished, and I return to the chalkboard. The students who are aware of the correct spelling, and there are a few, are eager to see their corrections be confirmed by me. For many others, their attempts have been serious ones, and they, too, await the outcome.

Making Children Feel Good About Their Spelling Attempts

"Okay, we know that there are three claps—*a part ment*," I begin. Pointing now to various individual letters in Lucas's version—*uportmit*—I say the three syllables slowly so that the dominant phonetic elements are obvious. "I see a lot of good sounds in Lucas's spelling. I can hear the *p*, the *r*, the *t*, the *m*, and the *t*. Good job, Lucas. I am glad that you circled this word, because there are some things that we can work on.

"I can see why Lucas started this word with the little word *up*. You can say the word and make it sound like it starts with an *up* at the beginning—*up art ment*. But that is not quite how we say it." I pronounce it the correct way.

Connecting the Unknown to a Word They Know

Quickly, I write the word *about* on the board. "Many of you know that this word is *about*. It has the same beginning sound as the word *apartment*. The *a* makes the *u* sound." And I write the first letter, *a*, directly underneath Lucas's version so that kids can easily compare the two.

"The next clap—*part*—has three big sounds: *p ar t*," I say. As I repeat this syllable, I write out the *p* and the *t* and leave a space in-between. "What letters are going to make the *ar* sound?"

Leah yells out, "*Car* is like *par*."

I copy *car* and underline the *ar*. "Leah remembered that *car* has the same sound as *par*." This is a simple review for most of my class. For some of my emerging spellers who might have guessed that the single letter *r* could make this *ar* sound, I glance in their direction to make sure that they are paying attention. "So far, we have *apart*. We're missing the last clap now—*ment*." Pointing once again to Lucas's version, *uportmit*, I put my hand over all the letters but the final *mit*. "Lucas, what does your word say at the end?"

He responds, "*Mit*."

Repeating the word, *a part ment*, I emphasize the final syllable, stretching it out for all to hear the *n* sound. Lucas recognizes the missing sound. To force another comparison, I quickly write *mint* and *ment*, one above the other, and tuck each word part into the total word: *apartmint* and *apartment*. "They both sound the same, don't they? It's one of those diction cases. Which one sounds correct?" The correct letters are filled in, and the word is now complete.

The final spelling always produces cheers from the class. Throughout the

lesson, I notice many of my first graders secretly changing their versions of the spelling as we make progress with the word. I really don't mind. It shows me that they are listening and keeping up with the lesson.

A Writer's Spelling Program

Children will grow as spellers when teachers support them as readers and writers (Bartch, 1992; Routman, 1991; Wilde, 1992; Stefano and Hagerty, 1985; Holdaway, 1979; Gentry, 1982; among many others). These educators that direct instruction in spelling must also regularly occur.

I continue to modify my spelling program to support my writing program. I have found no better way to assess a child's spelling ability than through authentic writing. This source of assessment is much more valuable to me than the traditional weekly spelling test. I remember the frustration of assigning lists of spelling words one week, witnessing their mastery on a Friday spelling test, and seeing these same words misspelled a week later on other assignments or in notes to friends. Spelling and writing were separate in students' minds.

Well, I still use spelling lists, but my lists are carefully constructed now to achieve specific purposes. After developing a totally individualized spelling program that had a lot of merits but was not very teacher-friendly, I returned to a formal weekly spelling list that's now the centerpiece of my spelling program.

The Weekly Spelling List

I used to resent the amount of time required to run a formal spelling program. The time taken for pre- and post-tests and for the student practice each week took time away from reading and our independent invitation writing time, which I believe are more worthy endeavors. Besides, with all the rich reading and writing in my class, my students were incidentally learning to spell. And so, one autumn four years ago, I decided to monitor my students' spelling growth through their journals and other informal assessment tasks and skip the weekly spelling routine altogether. Parents of my students understood my reasons and supported the shift.

After a semester away from the routine, I returned to it for two reasons: I missed the direct instruction in the classroom tied to each weekly category of words, and I missed the parents' assistance that accompanied the weekly spelling program. Most parents are knowledgeable about and comfortable with the traditional weekly spelling format. They understand that on Fridays their child will be taking a spelling test and that they can help him prepare. Practicing spelling words, whether in the class or at home, provides additional direct instruction in phonics and high-frequency words.

But I also knew that the prescribed lists could be ineffective. So, in returning to the weekly tests, I took a good, hard look at what I wanted. Rather than return to preselected lists from a published spelling program, I designed an "integrated spelling program" (Routman, 1992) that supported an already strong reading and writing program. I wanted my weekly spelling test to have

three strong ingredients: 1. a list of words that emphasize strong defining characteristics of phonics or word study; 2. some student self-selected words from the journals that individualize the program and reinforce the message that spelling has important ties to our writing; and, 3. a weekly review of first-grade fast words, some of which are irregular, combined with direct instruction in punctuation.

The Core Spelling List

Every week, I choose eight words that have common defining characteristics of spelling. I usually cull from spelling work I observe in the journals. For example, early in the year when I observe children confusing the *ch* and *sh* sounds, I divide my eight words so that the list is made up of words with the *ch* and *sh* spellings. This gives students plenty of practice during the week differentiating these sounds. I also deliberately select high-frequency words. I want children working with very common words. When I notice that many students are missing the common *oo* sound in words such as *pool, soon, moon,* and *fool,* I team up these four words with four words that have the *ee* sound, such as *sleep, keep, feet,* and *feed.* I don't want all eight words for the week to have the exact same rime. Experience has taught me that when all eight words have, for example, the same ending rime, students ignore the letter and sound relationships that make up the rime and rotely copy the collection of letters. Little learning takes place. I remember one student wrote the *-own* rime in a column on his test paper, and as I dictated each word, he simply wrote in the missing beginning sound. He had the system beat. Now, by mixing in at least two different elements, I'm assured that my students make some differentiation consciously.

Guess My Rule

ater in the year, the eight-word list is often developed by the class and me. Here is how one list arose from a shared-reading experience:

In late March, I announced that it was time to play "Guess My Rule," which is a fun word-study game. As a student reads aloud a big book story—one that we have read for enjoyment many times—I compile a list of words based on a common characteristic that I keep secret. Students have to guess what it is. The secret thread might be a common phonetic element: words with *er* spellings, *ing* endings, words with a *th* sound and/or spellings. Or the words I choose from the book might all be animal words, compound words, five-letter words, or "three-clap" (syllable) words.

On this day, the challenge was a little tougher. Borrowing a word-study strategy from First Steps (Heinemann, 1994), I selected from the book of nursery rhymes, *Time for a Rhyme,* words that contain the long *i* sound. Propping the big book of poems on the ledge of a chalkboard, a student read aloud "Little Miss Muffet," from which I chose first three words.

▲ *Reviewing a day's journal entry*

Little Miss Muffet sat on a tuffet
Eating her curds and whey.
Along came a spider and sat down beside her,
And frightened Miss Muffet away.

Guess My Rule

spider
beside
frightened

The children make some predictions about the secret rule. "Is it all the words with a *d* and an *e* in them?" one student asks.

"That is a good guess so far. Let's keep going and see if that is the rule." We continue on this way through "Twinkle Twinkle Little Star," "Little Boy Blue," "Hey, Diddle Diddle," and many more. Halfway through the book, the list has

grown, and still the children have not discovered the long *i* sound. I am not surprised, since some of the words on our list that make this sound do not even contain the letter *i*. To help them out, I read aloud the list of words, emphasizing the long *i* sounds. Children call out, "Long *i*, it's long *i*," thrilled to have figured out the rule and keep their "undefeated season" intact. We read the rest of the poems aloud, and the children scout ahead in search of more long *i* words.

Guess My Rule

spider	beside	frightened	white	I
cry	buy	ride	high	I'll
diamond	sky	like	drive	mice

To wrap up the lesson, I ask students if they notice any words on the list that could be grouped because of their spelling. The children mention many of the words ending in the letter *y* and the letter *e*.

The next time we meet, usually the next day at shared reading, I have the words written on notecards and taped to the chalkboard. I invite children to help me sort these words by common characteristics. We even provide a name for each list of words. And now our chart looks like this:

Guess My Rule

Quiet e	Y Makes the Long *i* Sound	-igh	Extra Words
beside	cry	frightened	I'll
white	buy	high	spider
ride	sky		
like			
drive			
mice			

At the end of the lesson, there are still words without a category. For now, we call them "extra words." We will explore them in a later lesson. Many children are not ready for this lesson to be over. They have thought of other words for the lists, and I invite them to add them.

Children will return to the lists at invitation time to make further additions. We talk about writing neatly. We also decide that these words cannot be "circled words." They must be spelled correctly on the list.

My spelling list the following week will be comprised of words from these lessons. I will pick four words from two different categories of words: *i* words with a *y* at the end and *i* words with a quiet *e*. I'll select words that have highest frequency of use in students' reading and writing. My next little-paper spelling lesson will also feature a word, not necessarily from these lists, that contains the long *i* sound. I am already curious to see what influence this lesson will have on their spelling attempts.

Self-Selected Journal Words

The final two words on the weekly spelling list—the ninth and tenth words—are different for each student. The children have selected them from among the words they've circled in their recent journal entries. I follow a "Have-a-Go" strategy that was originally introduced in Australia by Jo-Ann Parry and David Hornsby (*Write On: A Conference Approach to Writing*, Heinemann, 1988). In this method, children identify misspelled words from their daily writing and make an attempt, or have-a-go, at bringing these words to standard spelling.

Monday Selection

Children select their ninth and tenth spelling words on Mondays after journal writing. I encourage a parent to come in and help me with the process. After rereading their journal entry for the day, children select two of their circled words and copy them down just as they were developmentally spelled in their journal. In the next space, the children are encouraged to "try to fix" the spelling. Since the word was circled, there must be some part of it that is confusing to the child. This is where a new attempt must be made. When I or the parent volunteer checks in with each child, we watch for two things:

1. Students should choose appropriate words. If a student has misspelled high-frequency words, such as *were* or *that,* but selects *ocean liner* and *giraffe,* then I insist that the student change their ninth and tenth words. There is merit in selections made by the student, but the misspelling of high-frequency words must be given priority.

2. The try-to-fix words must be second attempts at the circled words. I want to see evidence of students' critical thinking. After the first few weeks, this usually is not a problem.

One-on-One Lessons

Next, the parent volunteer and I try to help the student reach a standard spelling for both selected words. This is an excellent opportunity to provide on-the-spot instruction in phonics and spelling strategies. An adult writes the standard spelling. Students are then given two notecards, on each of which they write their two words. They then place them in a library checkout envelope (which I've glued to the inside back cover of their journals at the beginning of the year). For the rest of the week, students pull out these cards to study the words individually or with a friend. On Friday after the test, each student hole punches these cards and puts them on a metal snap ring. This is their own personal collection of ring words, and it develops throughout the year.

▲ *A display of word sorts from students' private collections of ring words.*

Ring Words

The ring words have many uses. The children refer to them throughout the day. On a couple of occasions, students excitedly reached for their ring words during my demonstration lesson, calling out, "Oh, Mr. Henry, you don't have to circle that word. I have it on my ring!"

Word-sorting activities with the ring words serve as great review and offer excellent opportunities to "stimulate critical thinking and greater learning" (Zutell, 1993).

The Friday Test

At the onset of the Friday test, students take the "9 and 10 word" cards and place them facedown next to their test papers. After the first eight words are dictated to the class, I announce, "Okay, it is time for your ninth and tenth words. You may switch with your partner across or next to you." Many of the students remember their two extra words and write them down from memory. Other students take turns reading aloud their partner's words.

Sentence Construction, Punctuation, and First-Grade Fast Words: The Final Component of the Test

As the chart of first-grade fast words builds throughout the year, I rely on the Friday spelling test to reinforce them. Specifically, after students have done their

ten words, I dictate sentences for students to write that contain fast words. Children know I will be paying particular attention to capitals, periods, and spacing between words and letters. In the first four months of school, I dictate a single sentence. From then on, I include two sentences.

The spelling test is a perfect opportunity to assess these mechanical aspects of writing. It seems more appropriate to emphasize mechanics at this time so as not to inhibit authentic writing during journal-writing time.

Pretest

In any spelling program that I create, I try to follow a pretest–study–test method. With this method, students are given a pretest at the beginning of the week before these words are studied. Children correct their own pretests to clue them into the words that they will need to study before the final test.

There are still some aspects of my integrative spelling program that I am not satisfied with. While I am glad that children have individualized words that challenge them at their developmental spelling level, for a few children, two words are not enough. And I remain watchful that I don't develop a program that takes up too much time during the week to implement.

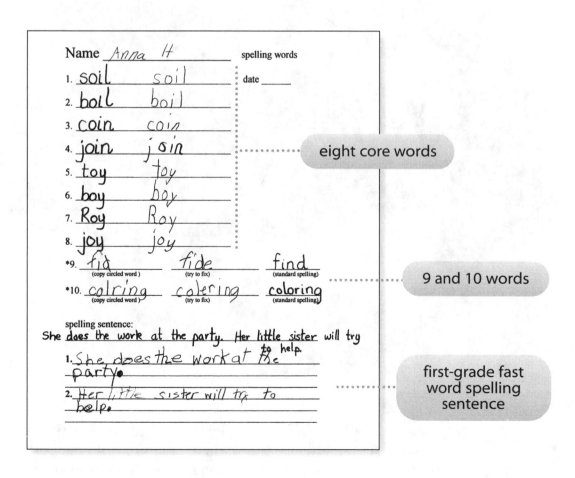

The Role of Journals in Exploring Writing Genres

Leah's first efforts at writing poetry.

The journal is a logical place for beginning writers to try their hand at writing poetry, fiction, number stories, and the other writing forms. During the early months of the year, I primarily model expository writing about events in my personal

life. Quite predictably, this is also the nature of the children's writing. But our regular shared-reading and -writing experiences eventually impact the children's journal writing. Students' experiments with new genres of writing begin to show up in the second half of the year. This delights me, as it attests to my students' curiosity about writing and their comfort level with the journal as a writing tool.

The Man with BIG Feet

There was once a man with BIG feet. But he was small. Everybody laughed at him. He was very sad. But one day a person said, "Why are you sad?" He said, everybody laughs at me." "I won't laugh at you." The end.

By Sarah Cohen ▶

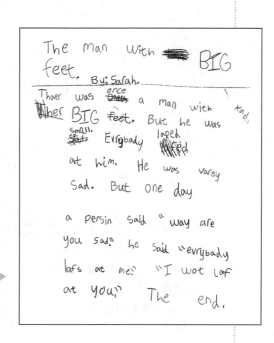

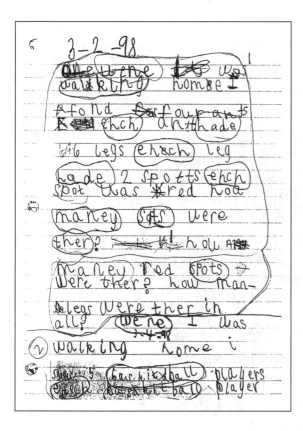

◀ When I was walking home I found four ants each ant had 6 legs. Each leg had 2 spots. Each spot was red. How many spots were there? How many red spots were there? How many legs were there in all?

By Corey B.

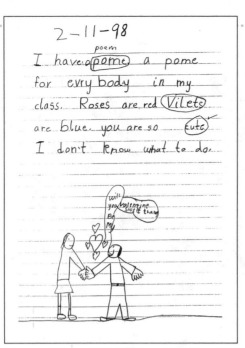

Roses are red
Violets are blue
You are so cute,
I don't know what to do.

By Marquez S.

I want to be a
scientist. I would
make crystals and
robots. I like
making stuff. It
is fun.

By Lucas C. ▶

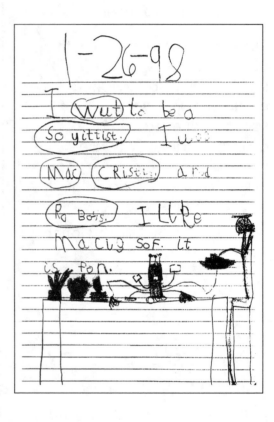

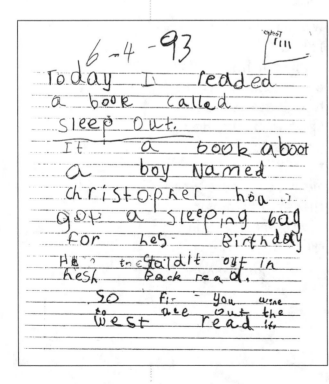

◀ Today I read
a book called
Sleep Out.
It [is] a book about
a boy named
Christopher who
got a sleeping bag
for his birthday
He slept out in
his back yard.
So if you want
to find out the
rest read it.

By Elizabeth F.

The Writing-Portfolio Checklist

A class-generated list of portfolio projects helps to keep students' independent writing efforts focused. I often use the criteria of our writing-portfolio checklist as a frame around the demonstration lessons I give, during which I foray into a new genre in my journal. The portfolio checklist is developed jointly by the class and me at the beginnings of the second and third trimesters.

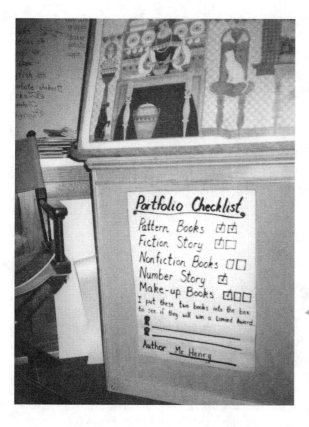

I keep my own chart-sized portfolio checklist (identical to the children's) posted at the back of the classroom, where all of our sharing takes place.

A Fiction-Writing Demonstration Lesson

Just as I do when drafting an expository journal piece in front of children, I purposely think out loud as I make the myriad decisions that go into a work of fiction. In this lesson, I model how a favorite author influences my own work. (We had just read the story *Where the Wild Things Are* by Maurice Sendak.)

Mr. Henry: Every time I read this book, I think that the writer, Maurice Sendak, must have had a blast writing it. Is this story fiction or nonfiction?

Taylor: Fiction. There's no such thing as those monsters….

Lindsay: And your room can't change into woods.

Mr. Henry: So, he got to make up these monsters any way he wanted. Now, we know that every good story has a problem. Did this story have a problem?

Josh: Yes. The little boy got in trouble and had to go to his room.

Mr. Henry: [pointing to my portfolio checklist and the empty checkoff box next to fiction story] On my portfolio checklist, I noticed that I haven't written a fiction story yet. I want to make an exciting story like Maurice Sendak did, but I don't want to make it just like his.

Matteo: You could make a girl getting into trouble instead.

Mr. Henry: No, I think I'm going to make it about two talking birds or maybe a cat that wants to be friends with a dog.

Lauren: You can make it about anything you want.

Mr. Henry: That's right!

The children help me make my writing decisions and unknowingly become more aware of their own writing options. At journal-writing next time, I'll begin the demonstration of fiction writing at the overhead projector with a review of this past discussion.

Portfolio Management

The students store portfolios (accordion folders), including mine, in two wooden boxes. The checklist is kept within the child's portfolio. It is each student's responsibility to check off projects as they are completed at invitation time. A seat-work folder kept in the child's seat pack holds projects they are currently working on. Children put completed projects on my chair at the back of the classroom. I check that the child has posted the finished date on the project and that he has listed the type of book that he completed from his portfolio checklist on the back cover of the book. This becomes another reminder to the students of their responsibilities to the checklist. At different times during the trimester, I have the children spread out all of their portfolio projects at their table and cross-check them with their checklist.

▲ *Lucas and Kevin collaborate on a fiction story.*

Introducing Fiction Writing

The Wild What If's
By Corey B.

What if school
was spelled like
this squwabas. Then
we would go to school
then just come back.
What if spiders
were chocolate ice cream.
Then we would be
looking for spiders
and we would [be] saying
I want spiders!

▶

A t various times during the year, I'll stand at the overhead projector and lead the children into the fiction genre by collaborating on "What if ..." scenarios. These are simple statements that stir children's imaginations. Looking out the window and watching the swirling

February snow, I'll ask, "What if the snow came down blue instead of white?" We delight in the fantastic ramifications of this event.

"We would have blue snowmen."

"The clouds would be blue."

"Your tongue would be blue when you eat the snow."

Some children will find this invitation to write "What if…" stories irresistible and will immediately write their own "What if…" tales during journal time.

Unlocking Writer's Block

Kevin was stumped as a writer. He was bothered that he spent so much time thinking of ideas while his peers seemed to be able to dive right into their writing. Kevin was turned on to "What if …" possibilities, and it broke the writing logjam for him.

What if… houses could talk and move? What if… animals could eat like people and the people could be the pets? What if… a polar bear could live in Florida? What if… every day one tooth would be loose? What if… people could fly and the animals that could fly didn't fly? What if… the moon was made out of cheese? What if… robots could do homework and job work too?

By Kevin G.

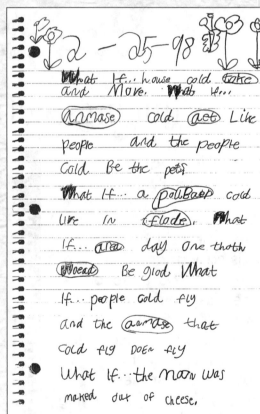

With encouragement, Kevin later expanded single "What if…" ideas from earlier writing into full journal entries.

What if people were made out of rubber. There would be no doctors. If people did not have bones you could change your face. If you did not have bones you could curl up into a pretzel and still be alive.

Cars would not be invented And instead of driving you would be bouncing. If you did not have bones you could melt into a puddle of skin. If you did not have bones, if [you] jumped up inside you would be going up and down very very fast up and down and you would be very dizzy.

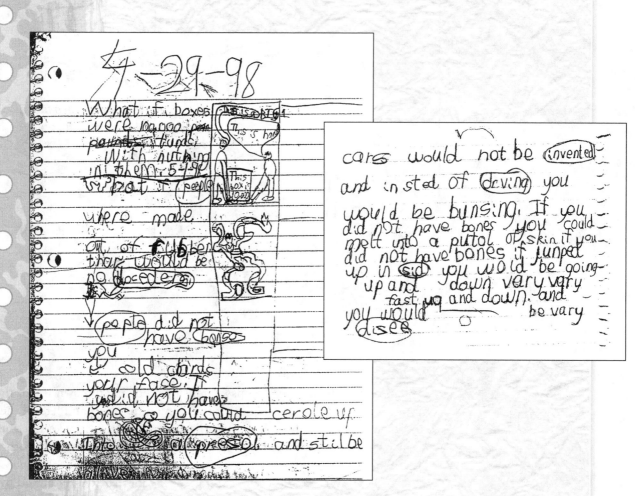

Using Story Maps

Before reading published fiction stories out loud, I ask the class questions that help them make predictions about the plot. For example, before reading *Miss Rumphius* by Barbara Cooney, I said, "Look at the cover of this book. I think the lady on this cover is Miss Rumphius. She doesn't look like she has a problem. I wonder what problem the author, Barbara Cooney, decided to make for this book. Let's read and find out."

I deliberately centered the discussion on the role of the writer and the choices she made. She, the author, invented the story problem. I want my students to see that they make these same decisions when they plan and write a story. To make it even clearer to children that they can construct their stories, much like an architect and carpenter might plan and build a house, I have them complete story maps before they begin writing. These maps, once done, provide a blueprint that guides their writing (see sample).

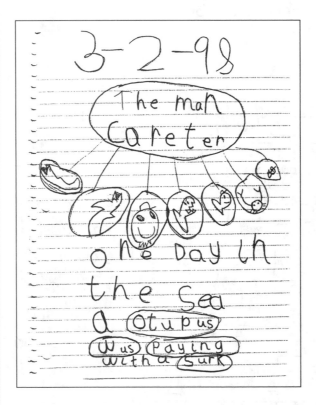

◀ *A student's first attempts at story mapping.*

Whether students use story maps or not, my modeling my own use of them sinks in. Detailed fiction stories are more common in the second half of the year. When I spot these first attempts at fiction by children, I make sure they receive a wide audience at sharing time. Often, this is all it takes to get other children to give the genre a try.

Here is how Avery used the safe confines of the journal-writing period to experiment with fiction writing:

The Magic Queen and the Tooth Fairy

This was the most
interesting day of the
Tooth Fairy life.
It was the 4 of
July and the
Tooth Fairy was
watching the fireworks.
The Tooth Fairy was
off from her job.
The fireworks
lasted long in to the
night and the Tooth
Fairy had to go to
bed.
In the night the Magic
Queen came and took
The Tooth Fairy.
She woke up and said,
"Where am I? You are
in the magic castle.
When they got to
[the castle] they went inside
and there was
magic everywhere.
After the Tooth
Fairy had stayed
at the castle for a
week, the Tooth Fairy
took the Magic Queen
to Tooth land.
The Magic Queen was
amazed. The tooth
Fairy and the Magic
Queen became good
friends. Then one night
The Magic Queen lost a tooth.
But when she woke up
she found 100 dollars
under her pillow. The
Magic Queen smiled.

The End

By Avery Glassman

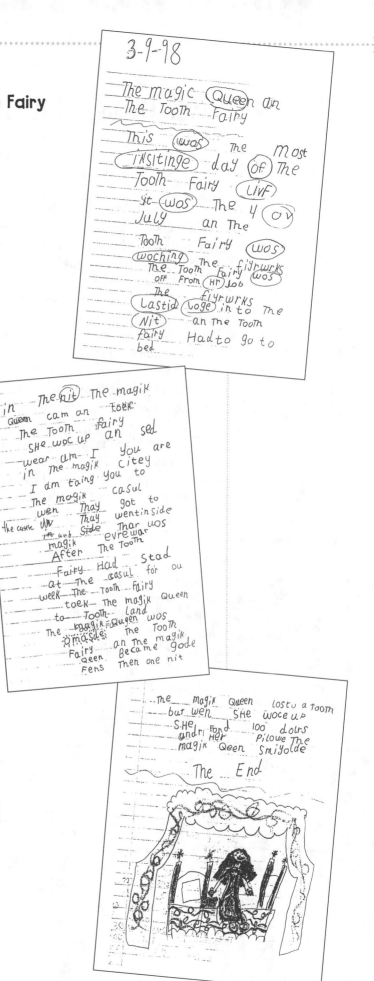

73

A Poetry Demonstraton

I begin to model poetry at the overhead projector late in the first semester. One April, inspired by the morning's activity with our weather chart, I decide to model a rhyming weather poem.

Drawing four writing lines on the transparency, I announce that I want to make a poem that has two words that rhyme with each other. The first word will be at the end of line two, and the second word will be placed at the end of line four. Then I begin. I stumble along and make plenty of mistakes (see illustration below). But I don't mind. As always, I want students to know that it is okay to make wrong turns with ideas and mechanical mistakes during drafting.

After finishing line four of the first stanza, "But snowy is feeling bad," I tell my students that we can't end the poem like that. I refer to the similar poem construction of "Frog's Lullaby," by Charlotte Pomerantz, hanging up in the classroom. With my pointer, I identify the characteristics of the two four-line stanzas of print. I suggest to the class that with two new words that rhyme, we can add another stanza to our poem. We continue until the bell rings, signaling the end of my writing time and the beginning of students' writing time.

Before setting the timer, I encourage children to try writing poems. Knowing how much the children love standing up in front of the class, I add, "And anyone who takes a try at writing a poem, I will let stand up and share at sharing time."

Sure enough, five students share their work (see next page).

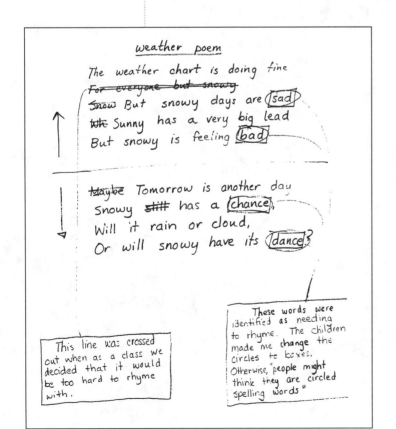

My rough draft of a shared writing lesson on poetry.

I love the weather in
The air, but I don't
Like rainy too much at
All. But beyond that
There's sunny so nice
And I like her warmness very
So. And I like her all over.

By Josh C. ▶

4-22-98

I love The weather in
the air but. I dont
like rainy to much
at all, but (beond) that
there's sunny so nice
and ~~youn~~ I ~~like~~ her~~warmnes~~ very
~~and~~ ~~her~~
So. I like all over.

4-22-98   (9 lines)

poem

Your hair is purple
your toes are pink
your eyes are blue
your nails are red
your Shirt is yellow
your legs are white
your head is brown
your bow is green
your arm is gray

Poem
Your hair is purple
Your toes are pink
Your eyes are blue
Your nails are red
Your shirt is yellow
Your legs are white
Your head is brown
Your bow is green
Your arm is gray.

By Anna M.

Sunny sunny in the air
Snowy is not there
But tomorrow is
Another day
Sunny might be away
Sunny might be wearing
Sunglasses.

By Lucas C. ▶

Current Events and Hamsters on the Loose: More Reasons for Journal Writing

The children will often break from whatever form of writing they are working on to write about something new that happens in the classroom. As I mentioned in Chapter 1, many times these events are staged to help out reluctant writers, but often they are not.

On our message/news board, I often read and post interesting newspaper clippings. Following a science unit on outer space, I brought in two different newspaper clippings about Saturn's largest moon and a large meteor that was considered to be on a dangerous path with Earth. For a few children, the topics were too irresistible not to write about at journal time.

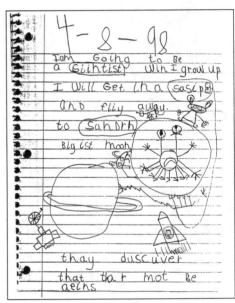

I am going to be
a scientist when I grow up.
I will get in a spaceship
and fly away
to Saturn's biggest moon.
They discovered
that there might be
aliens.

By Lucas C. ▶

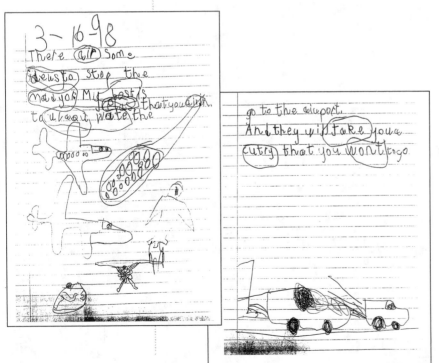

◀ There are some
ideas to stop the
meteor. My best is
to evacuate the
place that you are in.
Go to the airport.
And they will take you to a
country that you want to go.

By Matteo M.

I accidently left the top of a hamster's cage open after school one night. The children arrived the next morning to an empty hamster cage and a problem. How could we humanely trap our hamster and return him to his cage? Of course, my method of capture, which I explained in detail, was outlandish. (Let's just say it involved catapults) Through my example, children now understood that there were no limits to plans of their own.

Furball, the Missing Hamster
By Kevin G.

First you put some yummy stuff all around the room going to his cage. Then he will go into his cage. Then you put a book over his cage.

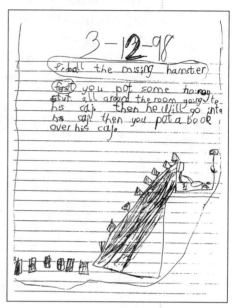

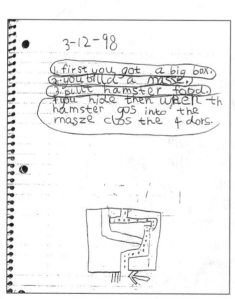

1. First you get a big box.
2. You build a maze.
3. Put [in] hamster food.
4. You hide. Then when the hamster goes into the maze, close the 4 doors.

By Steven L.

We have a missing hamster. What I would do is that I Will get a horseshoe Magnet and make him stick To it. "Now I gotcha."

By Marquez S.

Put food on the ground
until it gets three
or four feet away
from the shelf that
Furball's tank is on.
Then make stairs out
of books all
the way to
the top of Furball's
tank and [put] food
on the steps
that slides into Furball's cage.

By Josh C.

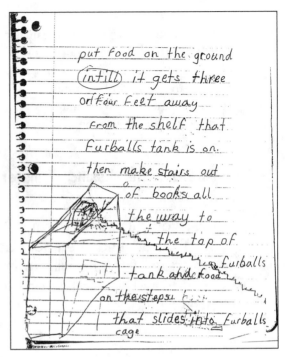

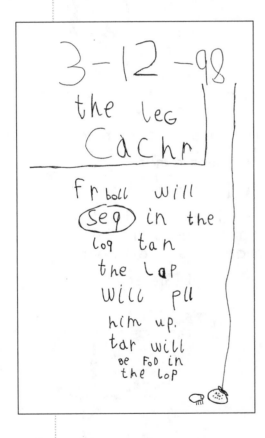

◀ **The Leg Catcher**
By Lucas C.

Furball will
step in the
loop then
the loop
will pull
him up.
There will
be food in
the loop.

I expose students to various genres of writing through my own writing demonstrations and through reading. Children also discover new writing topics through our daily content-area lessons. But if children are to grow as writers, then they need time to write. A journal-writing program that provides these regular opportunities to write and share, and so experiment, is essential.

CHAPTER 5

The Journal and Authentic Assessment

Throughout the year, I use the personal-writing journal as an authentic assessment tool for writing and spelling. The journal is used so regularly and comfortably by my students that it has become a reliable, or authentic, record of my students' writing and spelling development. The journal provides insight into the children's learning and important direction for my instruction. These spiral notebooks are used in formal, three-way

Evaluating students' journals provides me with valuable information about students' development as writers.

Authentic Assessment

Common assessment tools require regular instruction to come to a halt in order for the assessment to be taken. Friday spelling tests and end-of-a-unit math tests are two examples of this formal assessment. Authentic assessment makes these same judgments about learning as children apply their understandings in meaningful contexts. In other words, authentic assessments measure *during* learning performances.

▲ *Portfolio conferences allow students to celebrate their writing efforts with their parents.*

conferences between the child, parent, and me and, informally, when parents drop in to find out how their child is progressing. The journal is also used for children's self-assessment and self-guided learning. Throughout the year, children use their journals to select spelling words, and it is a source for writing ideas that are developed during our writer's workshop or invitation time. As their ability to write develops, it is common for individual children to request that certain journal entries be photocopied and taken home and shared with family.

Finally, I consult the journals regularly to prepare for whole-class and small-group spelling, writing, and reading lessons. Because journal writing is authentic, it is something that I can really count on to provide me with diagnostic information that informs my teaching.

In this chapter, I will look closely at two children, Taylor and Anna, students who began the year at different developmental levels of writing. As these two students develop as writers over the year, we will observe their progress through their journal writing and other informal-assessment classroom tools.

Taylor

I can usually tell which students have attended kindergarten in our school district. For most of my students, this is where journal writing begins. While there is variation—some teachers place a greater emphasis on drawing pictures before writing—most of my students have been exposed to independent writing at journal time by the time they arrive in my classroom. For Taylor, writing was a new experience. Early on, I met Taylor's grandmother, who is raising him. Looking back at his kindergarten experience,

she was not pleased. Taylor did not know all of his letters and was unaware of most beginning sounds. When I shared with her Taylor's beginning journal entries for the year—random letters with my accompanying transcription written next to his text—she looked at me with an uneasy, questioning glance.

Taylor's 9-4-97 journal entry

I love Bob. He's our best friend.

Taylor is at a beginning stage of writing. His use of random letters over made-up squiggles and marks shows that he has ideas for using the alphabet. I am excited that Taylor is even writing. Writers in these early stages often are hesitant to even put the pencil to the paper. Today, my demonstrations helped him in choosing a writing topic, as we both wrote about the classroom pet Bob the Box Turtle.

Taylor's 9-22-97 entry
I have a haircut.

Taylor's 9-24-97 entry
I saw a star. It was brightly And it was nice.

In both of these early-year entries, Taylor shows a developing awareness of writing mechanics. In both examples, my earlier demonstration lessons at the overhead projector impacted Taylor's writing. In the first example, I modeled using my fingers to "plant" spaces between words. When I stopped at Taylor's desk to take his dictation, he proudly shared with me evidence of the same: "I left some room—see, a space."

Taylor is immersed in his journal.

In the second entry, Taylor experiments with periods. Again, my demonstration lesson impacted Taylor's writing. During that lesson, I purposely left out all ending punctuation. Later, while rereading, we discussed the problems with meaning that resulted from the absence of punctuation marks. However, in later journal entries, Taylor would not be consistent in his experimental use of both capitals and periods and spacing between words. There would be days of use and nonuse. I do not worry. With regular doses of teacher modeling and the accompanying opportunities to write, Taylor will show a greater understanding of the tools of the writer.

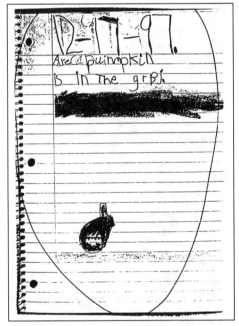

Taylor's 12-10-97 entry
I have a baby
brother. I play with
him.

Taylor's 12-17-97 entry
Our pumpkin
is in the garbage.

Both of these December entries show that in the last couple of months, Taylor has made strong gains in his writing. Taylor is becoming a very confident writer. I remember days when Taylor struggled to think of topics for writing. This rarely happens now.

There are big improvements noticeable in his writing mechanics. Taylor regularly spaces between words. His handwriting is improving. In the first entry, Taylor interprets the two words *play with* as a single, multisyllable word, *playwith*, and writes *plw*. This is common for beginning writers, and I am not concerned. I am pleased to see many of the beginning and strong consonant sounds of words show up in his writing. His spelling of *garbage* (*grbj*) and *baby* (*beb*) shows that he is attending to more than just the beginning and ending sounds of words. He is also beginning to use vowels in his developmental spelling of words. Taylor is developing a sight-word writing vocabulary with his successful use of first-grade fast words in his writing. I will look for this to continue. The proper spelling of *brother* means that he is likely consulting the word wall and/or our class list of family words.

While I am pleased with Taylor's development thus far, demonstration lessons that follow will speak to the following concerns:

◎ Taylor appears content at this point to write one idea and fill the remaining time with illustrating. I want to make sure that he is aware of how single ideas can be developed. I will model this at the overhead projector and point out how other authors, both in our class and in the literature within the class, have done so.

◎ Some of Taylor's words—*have* spelled *hys*, *him* spelled *hena*—are missing some obvious, strong, phonetic sounds. Outside of seeing the standard spelling of these words, I would prefer to see *have* and *him* spelled something closer to *hav*, *hv*, and *hm*, *hem*. I will emphasize the heavy dominant consonants in modeling, during whole-class spelling lessons and in reading groups.

These targeted lessons for Taylor fit the needs of many students in the class.

▲ *Taylor shares a book with friends.*

Taylor's 3-23-98 entry

I saw Steven on
Wednesday. He said
Hi. I said hi too.
And he saw my dog.

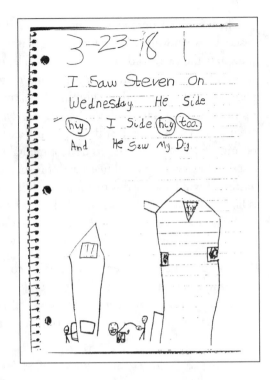

Taylor is a confident writer. He informs me that his grandmother tells him all the time how good a writer and reader he has become. He often takes advantage of my offer to photocopy journal-writing pages to share with family at home.

Taylor continues to build his sight-word vocabulary. He shows that he understands the purpose of circling words—the acknowledgement that a spelling is probably incorrect. Taylor regularly writes more than a single idea for each entry. His handwriting and spelling are very readable. Capitalization is still confusing. Punctuation marks are no longer placed randomly but follow complete ideas. As I move the writing time from 15 to 20 minutes, I will look for the amount of Taylor's writing to increase.

Taylor's 4-29-98 through 5-8-98 entries

Me and Katy All Day
1. Taylor was fast
asleep then a noise
outside woke
Taylor up. Taylor
opened the door then
nothing was there.
2. Friday was a
nice day. Katy came
out of her house
and went to
Taylor's house.
He woke up and Katy

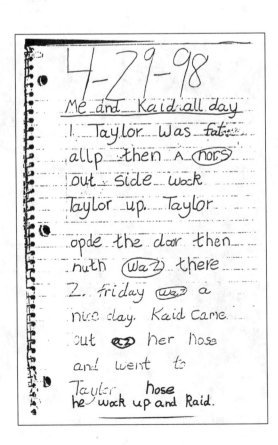

was sitting on the foot
of Taylor's bed.
3. Saturday was a snow day.
I went over [to] Katy's house.
She was asleep.
The doorbell rang.
She opened the door.
4. Sunday was a
snowing day.
Katy stayed home.
And I stayed home
too.
He woke up and he
looked out side.
"Ho," said Taylor.
5. Friday was spring.
I woke up and he
looked outside. He ran
outside.

Taylor is very proud of his chapter book. This is one of Taylor's first forays into fiction writing. He points out several times during this weeklong effort at writing how he continues to add to his story each day.

Many of the invitation-time projects that are read aloud during sharing time in the spring originate from journal-writing entries. Taylor looks forward to sharing this work with others.

Taylor's book ideas piggyback from another child's adaptation of *Frog and Toad All Week* by Arnold Lobel. There is a lot to be excited about with Taylor's writing. It is nice to see some voice emerge in his writing. He experiments with quotation marks for the first time. His writing is logically sequenced. Writing mechanics continue to improve. His sight-word writing vocabulary continues to grow. I am dismayed, however, that he continues to misspell high-frequency fast words, such as *of* (*as*), *was* (*waz*), and *house* (*hose*). I'll have to make sure that some of these high-frequency words becomes 9 and 10 spelling words. I will also have to follow up with his journal writing at sharing time and help him account for his spelling correctly the first-grade fast words. His use of vowels in his writing is much stronger. It does not surprise me that Taylor's reading has also made tremendous gains during this same time frame.

My Goals for Taylor

Taylor needs to spend the final month of school writing as much as possible. Feedback from his peers and me must encourage his efforts. Taylor is also ready to notice more variations in vowel patterns. "Why do some words have quiet *e*'s at the end and some do not?" Taylor also fails to account in his writing for all of the phonetic sounds that make up many words that he uses. When he writes *allp* for *asleep*, there is no attempt to account for the *s* or long *e* sound in the

word. Similarly for *stayed* (*sad*), *Friday* (*frid*), and *looked* (*loot*). Again, many of the strong consonant sounds of these words are missing. Further lessons will take place in the whole class, small groups, or individually when Taylor seeks me out on his own for help.

One strategy for drawing attention to the missing sounds in these words is to isolate on paper or on an individual chalkboard the standard and the child's developmental spelling of these words. After consulting student journals, where my list of word pairs is generated, a sample dialogue in small groups or individually follows:

1. Friday   2. frid

Mr. Henry: Which word spells *Friday*, number one or number two?

Taylor: Number one. [Often, the child knows right away which is the correct spelling when faced with such a glaring discrepancy. But I continue and push him to account for the difference.]

Mr. Henry: Let's say the word *Friday* together—*Fri-day*. How many claps [syllables] does it have?

Taylor: Two.

Mr. Henry: How do you know that number two cannot be *Friday*?

Taylor: It doesn't have the *day* sound.

Anna

Every year, I have a few students like Anna in my class. She arrives in first grade already reading and, as the beginning entry in her journal (see below) shows, she also has advanced skills in writing.

After talking with her parents, I discover that Anna has a late-September birthday and is the youngest in my class. However, I am not surprised to learn that Anna is surrounded at home with books and with family members who read and value literacy. Her early interests in reading and writing have been encouraged. It is no wonder that she entered public school already, as Frank Smith would say, a "junior member" of the Literacy Club (Smith, 1988).

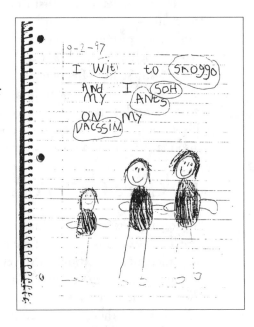

Anna's 9-2-97 journal entry

I went to Chicago
And I saw
my Aunts
on my
vacation.

▲ *Anna shares her journal with box turtles Bob and Martha.*

Anna's beginning fall journal entry is very strong. She understands a lot about writing. Her first entry is readable by me. Anna reflects on a special memory from the summer and is proud to share it with her classmates and me. Anna has a beginning writing vocabulary, and she is not afraid to take chances with new words that she does not know how to spell. Anna demonstrates good phonics skills. She attends in her spelling to the beginning, middle, and ending sounds. She understands the importance already of vowels in spelling. I do not usually see such a consistent use of vowels until later in the year.

My Goals for Anna

I know that Anna attends to my demonstration lessons at the overhead projector. Her quick understanding and use of circled spelling words proves that. My early goals for Anna, based on this entry and her other beginning entries, are as follows:

◎ Keep Anna writing. She is off to a great start. I want her to know how pleased I am with her effort. Even with all the time that I must spend with my struggling writers, I will have to provide time for Anna to share her writing with me.

◎ Help Anna understand that her writing does not have to end after one complete idea or sentence is written down. She has established an early format of writing during journal time. She spends just enough time writing to record one idea. The remainder of the time is spent illustrating. Her work is always contained on a single page of her spiral notebook. Anna needs to see me write multiple ideas and use more than a single page of journal paper at one journal time period.

◎ Anna is ready to use the classroom as a resource for her writing. Early in the year, the class is barren of charts and student work. The fast-words chart has few or no words. As the classroom walls come alive with the products from our shared-reading and -writing activities, Anna will incorporate their use into her writing.

Anna's 9-12-97 entry ▶

Good bye, Jake

I will miss you
I hope you will
have a party
with your
friends
and your
parents.

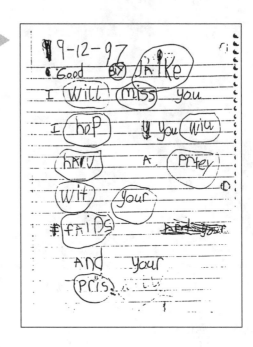

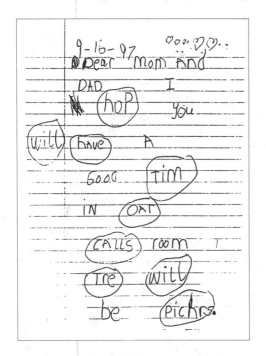

◀ Anna's 9-16-97 entry

Dear Mom and
Dad I
hope you
will have a
good time
in our
class room.
There will
be pictures.

In both entries, Anna is writing a letter. In the first letter, she is saying good-bye to our class snake, Jake. Jake the Garter Snake briefly visited the class before he was let go so that he could prepare for winter hibernation. On his last day, he received many copies of journal entries written by the students.

The second entry was a letter written to her mom and dad, welcoming them to the classroom at Open House. Her parents' response, written later that night, follows. Authentic letters written by the children to friends and family are a great motivational tool to get children writing.

Anna's parents respond in Anna's journal at Open House; Anna shares her portfolio with her mom.

Anna Explores Other Genres

Anna is spending less and less time illustrating and more time writing. As she adds details to her writing, she includes more than one idea in her writing. Anna consistently punctuates her entire entry every day with a single period placed at the end of her writing.

Before I expect the children to attempt a new genre of writing, I model the process. Often, I use the modeling time at the overhead projector to do so. Anna enjoys these challenges of leaving her daily-event writing and attempting alternative writing options that I make available to her. Here are her first attempts at writing a book review and a "What if ..." story:

Anna's 1-21-98 entry

I like this book
that is called
My New Kitten.
I like how they
did the pictures
of the kittens.
I liked it very much.

Anna's 2-27-98 entry

What if crayons
were made out of
candy? What if
wood was made
out of grass.
What if books
were made out
of lunchboxes.
What if air
were made
out of candy.

2-27-98
What if crayons
were made out of
candy? what if
wood was made
out of grass.
What if books
were made out
of lunchboxs.
What if air
were made
out of candy.

I make special efforts to stop at Anna's table to provide encouragement and motivation. Sometimes, it is a gentle pat on her back and a few whispered words: "Anna, you are like a writing machine. You have so much to say." Other times, I offer advice and prompting to try a new genre of writing recently introduced to the class.

Anna's journal entries show that she is more effective in her use of punctuation marks. During a shared-writing experience, the class helped me to write a pattern book. I explained that titles of books are often underlined when they are written down. Anna demonstrates her understanding of this. Anna's journal has become an important assessment tool to explain progress that she is making in all her writing.

Anna spends no time illustrating in her journal anymore. She is proud of the volume of her writing as she records and circles at the top of her journal how many lines of writing she completes on the page. Anna continues to circle words where there is some doubt about the spelling.

Anna's 4-27-98 entry

Yesterday I went to the Science center with my Mom and my brother. I bought a keychain and an airplane pin that sparkles. I got a pencil that sparkles too. I also got a pen that is purple and it has different colors in it when you turn it. At McDonald's I got a gorilla with its baby. The next time she goes to Sam's Club she is going to get Flubber the movie.

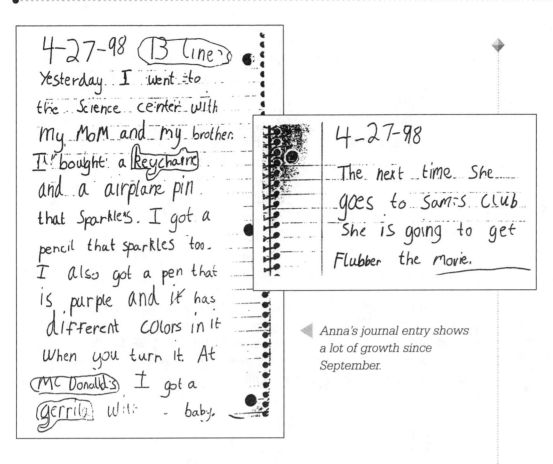

4-27-98 (13 Lines)
Yesterday. I went to the Science center with my Mom and my brother. I bought a Keychain and a airplane pin that Sparkles. I got a pencil that sparkles too. I also got a pen that is purple and it has different colors in it when you turn it. At McDonald's I got a gerrila with - baby.

4-27-98
The next time She goes to Sam's Club She is going to get Flubber the movie.

Anna's journal entry shows a lot of growth since September.

Anna has made a lot of progress since early September. But her writing gains are a result of much more than the demonstration lessons that I provide prior to each journal-writing session. Anna is a reader who has regular opportunities to read. The print-rich classroom and choice available to Anna through our writer's workshop or invitation time encourage Anna to explore literature. Her experimentation and curiosity with her writing results in constructive gains.

The great range of abilities between students like Taylor and Anna in one classroom starting as early as the first grade used to amaze me. Now I know it is typical of any classroom. How well we are able to meet the individual needs of every child determines how successful our model of instruction is. Journal writing offers the opportunity to tie powerful direct instruction with assessment and meet the needs of the whole class.

Other Assessment Tools

There are other tools that I use throughout the year that help me assess the children's writing and spelling. Many of these same tools serve as writing resources for the children and impact their journal writing.

20 Words That Tell a Story

Four or five times during the year, I administer a 20-word, unannounced spelling/phonics check to the class, which provides feedback to my teaching and

assessment information for the parents of my class. The set of 20 circled words selected over the years from the children's journals is not that easy.

1. little	11. look
2. they	12. went
3. what	13. this
4. there	14. because
5. with	15. why
6. said	16. down
7. people	17. have
8. from	18. does
9. play	19. you
10. some	20. about

Many people might argue that they are not first-grade words but second- and third-grade words. They do not all follow strict phonetic rules. These 20 words are high-utility speaking and writing words. And they will see these words over and over again in their reading. I considered using the 20 Grade One Words from The Gentry Spelling Grade Level Placement Test (Gentry, 1997):

1. all	11. one
2. me	12. be
3. do	13. like
4. come	14. am
5. play	15. you
6. at	16. see
7. yes	17. is
8. on	18. ten
9. the	19. was
10. and	20. no

Instead, though, I decided to build a list of words that had more elements of phonics and word study. It seemed such a list would be an effective assessment tool.

I purposely do not tell children or their parents what the words are nor when the assessment will be made. As often happens with spelling tests, I do not want the words memorized just for the test. While the rest of the class works at their seats, I ask five children at a time to come up to my reading table, and I administer the check. I avoid whole-class testing. I want the close proximity to the students. I want to make sure that they attend to the task so that the results are valid. Also, a nurturing hand is needed, especially early in the year, when the children are faced with the awesome task of trying to spell all of these words correctly.

They need to know that I do not expect mastery. I am interested in their attempts. The first try is given early in the year. After that, I retest at the end of each quarter or trimester. At the end of the year, the set of tests tell quite a story of spelling, phonics, and handwriting development. Any conference that I have with parents or teachers about the child often begins with these tests.

The number of correct responses is tallied and circled at the top of each paper. However, often the real tale of growth is revealed through their errors. Taylor's four tests arranged together follow:

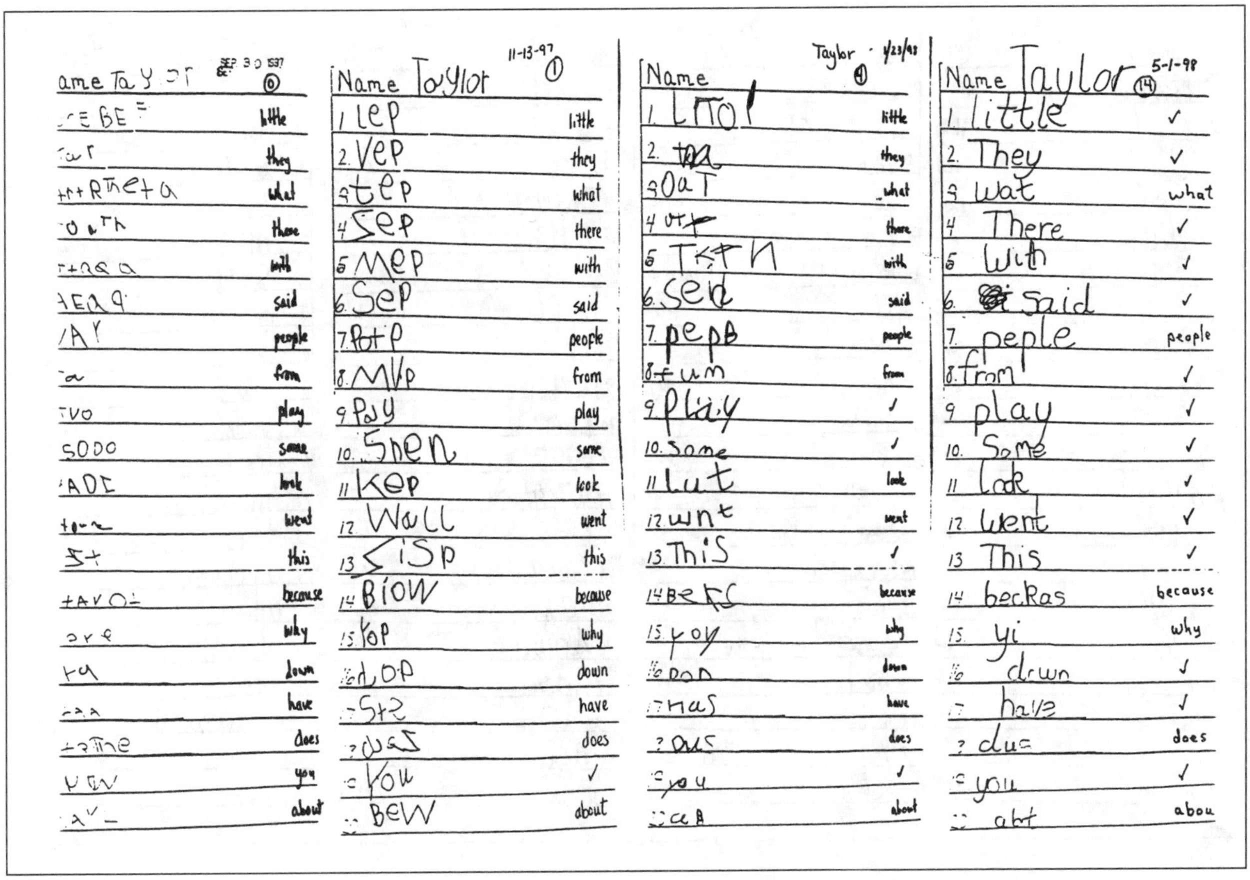

The handwritten spelling tests appear in four columns at the top of the page.

Column 1 (SEP 30 '97):

ame Ta y ɔ r	
ˤ ᴇ ᛒᴇ ᶠ	little
ᶠu r	they
ᴛᴛᴛ R ᵀʰᴇ ᵗ a	what
ᶠ0 ⌄ ᵀ᷂	there
ᵀᴛᴅᴇ a	with
ᵀ ᴇᴅ ᵍ	said
˸ A ʸ	people
˸ a	from
ᴛ V 0	play
5 0 D 0	some
ᴬᴅᴱ	look
ᵗ ᴑ ᵐ	went
ᴊ ᵗ	this
ᵗ A V 0 ˸	because
ᴐ ᵛ ᴇ	why
ᵗ ᴾᴨ	down
ᴖ ᴬ ᴠ	have
ᵗ ᴬ ᵀ ᴴᴇ	does
V ᴇ V	you
ᴬ ᵛ	about

Column 2 (11-13-97, ①):

Name Taylor	
1. LeP	little
2. VeP	they
3. teP	what
4. SeP	there
5. MeP	with
6. SeP	said
7. PotP	people
8. MVP	from
9. PdJ	play
10. Snen	some
11. KeP	look
12. Wall	went
13. ∫iSp	this
14. BiOW	because
15. KoP	why
16. dOP	down
17. -St2	have
18. 2uS	does
19. You	✓
20. BeW	about

Column 3 (Taylor · 1/23/98, ④):

Name	
1. LTO	little
2. tea	they
3. OaT	what
4. vt	there
5. TKTN	with
6. Seb	said
7. PePB	people
8. Fum	from
9. Play	✓
10. Sone	✓
11. Lut	look
12. wnt	went
13. This	✓
14. BeKS	because
15. Yoy	why
16. DoD	down
17. THaS	have
18. QuS	does
19. you	✓
20. aB	about

Column 4 (Taylor, 5-1-98, ⑭):

Name Taylor	
1. little	✓
2. They	✓
3. wat	what
4. There	✓
5. With	✓
6. said	✓
7. peple	people
8. from	✓
9. play	✓
10. Some	✓
11. Lok	✓
12. Went	✓
13. This	✓
14. beckas	because
15. yi	why
16. drwn	✓
17. have	✓
18. duc	does
19. you	✓
20. abt	abou

Taylor's 4 Tests

It would be easy to look at Taylor's first attempt and be overwhelmed by all the deficiencies in his performance. I choose instead to concentrate on the strengths. First, I am impressed that Taylor attempted all the words. Often, I am faced with a lot of empty spaces on his initial efforts in the fall. Second, even though Taylor uses random letters and shows no understanding of beginning and ending sounds, I am encouraged that he is using mostly letters and not made-up squiggles and marks.

As the year progresses, it is easy to note progress. In the November and January trials, Taylor exhibits a growing understanding of beginning and ending sounds. By the beginning of May, Taylor has mastered 70% of the words. Even his errors are very phonetic.

Anna's story, as revealed through her four phonics/spelling samples, is much different (see next page).

From the beginning, Anna's use of vowels in her spelling is impressive. Far from a random use, her location and choice of vowels in the words are advanced. During the year, the different spelling attempts show a growing understanding of spelling and phonics rules. This development matches a similar growth in her journal. Test results from the whole class inform my journal demonstration lessons. They also impact the words that I choose for little-paper spelling lessons and chalkboarding circled words.

 Taylor's spelling tests from September to May

#	SEP 28 97		11-10-97		Anna H. 1-29-98		5-7-98	
1	litte	little	LittL	little	Little	✓	little	✓
2	Teay	they	they	✓	Thay	they	they	✓
3	Went	what	want	what	what	✓	what	✓
4	her7	there	ther	there	There	✓	ther	✓
5	With	✓	Wich	✓	With	✓	wilth	✓
6	Sed	said	Secid	said	Siekd	said	Said	✓
7	PePL	people	PePL	people	peple	people	pepole	people
8	Furm	from	From	✓	From	✓	from	✓
9	PhLY	play	PLay	✓	play	✓	play	✓
10	Saum	some	Some	✓	some	✓	Some	✓
11	Look	✓	Look	✓	Look	✓	look	✓
12	Went	✓	Went	✓	went	✓	went	✓
13	Tish	this	The	this	This	✓	this	✓
14	becas	because	becaus	because	because	✓	because	✓
15	Uly	why	Wiay	why	wye	why	Why	✓
16	danwn	down	down	down	down	✓	down	✓
17	hau	have	have	✓	have	✓	have	✓
18	dass	does	duss	does	dows	does	does	✓
19	You	✓	You	✓	you	✓	you	✓
20	Abt	about	abotet	about	abot	about	About	✓

▲ *Anna's spelling tests from September to May*

"Help Me" Books

As the year progresses, the volume of the children's writing increases. Children become more aware of spelling concerns. Children ask me how to spell words after journal writing ends and during the time between reading groups. I used to just tell them. Then I realized that by not making them first attempt the word on their own, I was missing an opportunity for them to construct new understandings about spelling from their prior ideas about phonics and word study. In other words, I wasn't letting them learn from their mistakes. So next, I had students get a scrap piece of paper, write the word, and bring it up to me. Using their attempt, I concentrated on what they knew about the word, much like a lesson-in-the-margin, and I helped them come to a standard spelling. The scrap piece of paper was then thrown away, and the child returned to her writing.

It occurred to me that tossing out these scrap papers wasn't wise. I was essentially discarding important assessment information and authentic student-spelling resources. And so, with the help of construction paper, plain white paper, and a stapler, "Help Me" books were born. The children labeled and decorated their covers. The children now make all of their first attempts at spelling in these booklets.

Where Most Students Stand

The Help Me book is a great resource to share with parents during conferences. It provides rich information that helps me determine where a student lies on the spelling developmental continuum. I can often tell through the Help Me books what direction to take with my spelling instruction.

By the end of the year many of my students still have unresolved punctuation issues. They are comfortable using periods and capitals but their usage is not always correct. For most students, knowledge of common spellng patterns helps them decode unknown words. Most students will master 75% of the list of 20 words. But all of the children by the end of the year are comfortable writing independently for 15-20 minutes daily. This comfort level with writing will serve them well in the years ahead, helping them to build new understandings about conventions and mechanics as they develop their own writer's voice.

Closing Reflections

My journal-writing story is about efforts to get children excited about writing. It is also about moving journals away from being just another routine activity. Journals can be that meaningful enterprise, given the right conditions. Every year, it's a struggle. Often, the problems that arise are familiar, and I know what I am to do. Many times, they are not, and I search for answers. I remember when Lucas excitedly came into the classroom one morning, eager to share a tale about his trip to the grocery store the previous evening. He had stumbled upon a school-supplies section of the market, where he saw 90-page notebooks for sale. "Mr. Henry, I know what I am writing about today. We found journals. Hundreds of them!"

If I am listening, the children usually let me know how I am doing. And with a long career of going to school ahead for my students, it's important that these first steps be successful ones.

Bibliography

Journal Articles and Professional Books Cited

Adams, M.J. *Beginning To Read.* Cambridge, MA: Harvard University Press, 1990.

Bartch, Judi. "An Alternative To Spelling: An Integrated Approach." *Language Arts* Vol. 69. (Oct. 1992.) pp 404-408.

Brooks, Jacquelin and Martin. *In Search of Understanding: The Case for Constructivist Classrooms.* Alexandra, VA. Association for Supervision and Curriculum Development, 1993.

Cambourne, Brian. *The Whole Story: Natural Learning and the Acquisition of Literacy in the Classroom.* Auckland, New Zealand: Ashton Scholastic, 1988.

Chall, J. *Learning to Read: The Great Debate.* New York: McGraw-Hill, 1967.

DiStefano, Philip P. and Patricia Hagerty. "Teaching Spelling at the Elementary Level: A Realistic Perspective." *The Reading Teacher.* (January, 1985.)

Education Department of Western Australia. *First Steps Writing Developmental Continuum.* Portsmouth, NH: Heinemann, 1994.

Fitzgerald, J. *The Teaching of Spelling.* Elementary English 30:79-84. 1953.

Frank, Michael. "Tell It All to A Friendly Diary: Four Centuries of Intimate Thoughts." *The New York Times,* May 16, 1997.

Gentry, Richard. "An Analysis of Developmental Spelling in GYNS AT WRK." *The Reading Teacher.* Vol 36 (Nov. 1982) pp. 191-192.

Holdaway, Don. *The Foundations of Literacy.* Auckland, New Zealand: Ashton, Scholastic. 1979.

Montgomery, M. *The Test-Study Method Versus the Study-Test Method of Teaching Spelling In Grade Two: Study II.* Unpublished Master's Thesis, University of Texas, 1957.

Parry, Jo-Ann and David Hornsby. *Write On: A Conference Approach to Writing.* Portsmouth, NY: Heinemann, 1988.

Routman, Regie. *Invitations.* Portsmouth, NH: Heinemann, 1991.

Smith, Frank. *Joining the Literacy Club.* Portsmouth, NH: Heinemann, 1988.

Strickland, Dorothy. "Educating African American Learners At Risk: Finding A Better Way." *Language Arts.* 1971. pp. 328-335.

Wilde, Sandra. *You Kan Red This!* Portsmouth, NH: Heinemann, 1992.

Yee, A. "Is the Phonetic Generalization Hypothesis in Spelling Valid?" *Journal of Experimental Education* 37: pp. 82-91. 1969.

Zutell, Jerry. Conference Papers: *Literacy for the New Millenium.* Melbourne, Australia: Australian Reading Association, First International Conference and 19th National Conference, World Congress Center, July, 1993.

Children's Books Cited

Barrett, Judi and Ronald. *Animals Should Definitely Not Wear Clothing.* New York: Scholastic, 1970.

Cooney, Barbara. *Miss Rumphius.* New York: Viking, 1982.

Cowley, Joy. *Yuck Soup.* Bethel, WA: The Wright Group, 1986.

DePaolo, Tomie. *Bill and Pete.* New York: Putnam and Grosset Book Group, 1978.

Gardner, Margorie, Heather Philpot, and Jane Tanner, illustrators. *Time For A Rhyme.* Crystal Lake, IL: Rigby, 1982.

Lobel, Arnold. *Frog and Toad All Week.* New York: HarperCollins, 1976.

Pomerantz, Charlotte. "Frog's Lullaby," from *All Asleep* by Charlotte Pomerantz, illustrated by Nancy Tafuri. New York: Greenwillow Books, 1984.

Rigby, Education. *The Trolley Ride.* 1984.

Sendak, Maurice. *Where the Wild Things Are.* New York: HarperCollins, 1964.

Teague, Mark. *The Field Beyond the Outfield.* Scholastic, 1992.